Imaginative Imagery
Set Your Imagination Free
by Jennie Hennesay
Copyright 2016

This Book is dedicated to my five wonderful children who each took that arduous journey into adulthood, developed their own individuality and talents and proudly display them. They taught me it's OK to be who you are and that you don't need to do what everybody else is doing. It took me a long time to accept that, and there are times I realize I'm slipping back into the old habits. They're still there leading the way and setting the example. Backward isn't it? Well, that's me. Born breech and have been backward ever since.

So many people have guided me along this journey to mention them all, but I'd like to thank Marilyn Southmayd for helping me get this book published.

A special thanks to Becky C. Alexander and Kim Vee and all the wonderful colorists in their Facebook groups for the inspiration, guidance and encouragement they've provided.

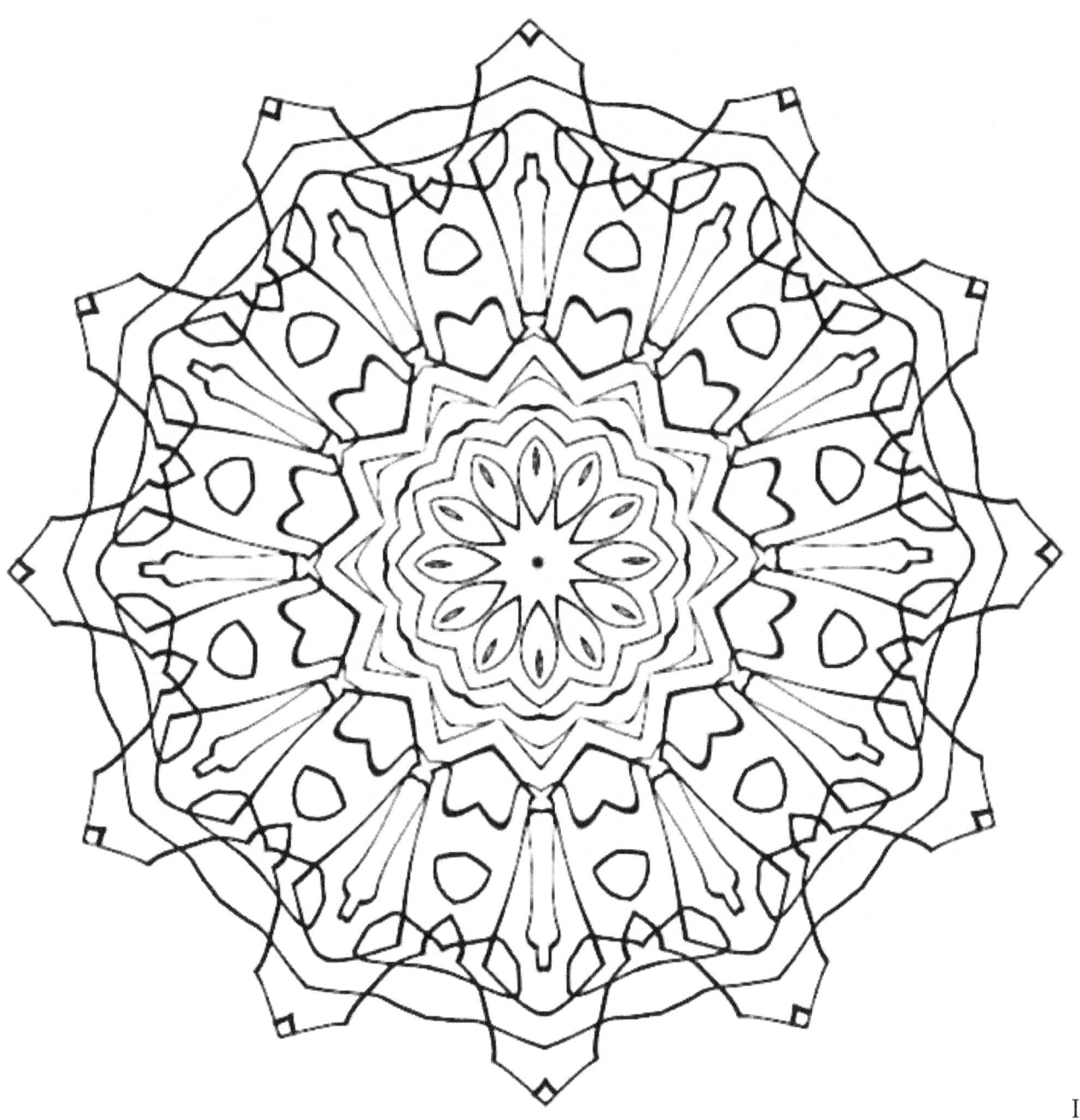

Bakery

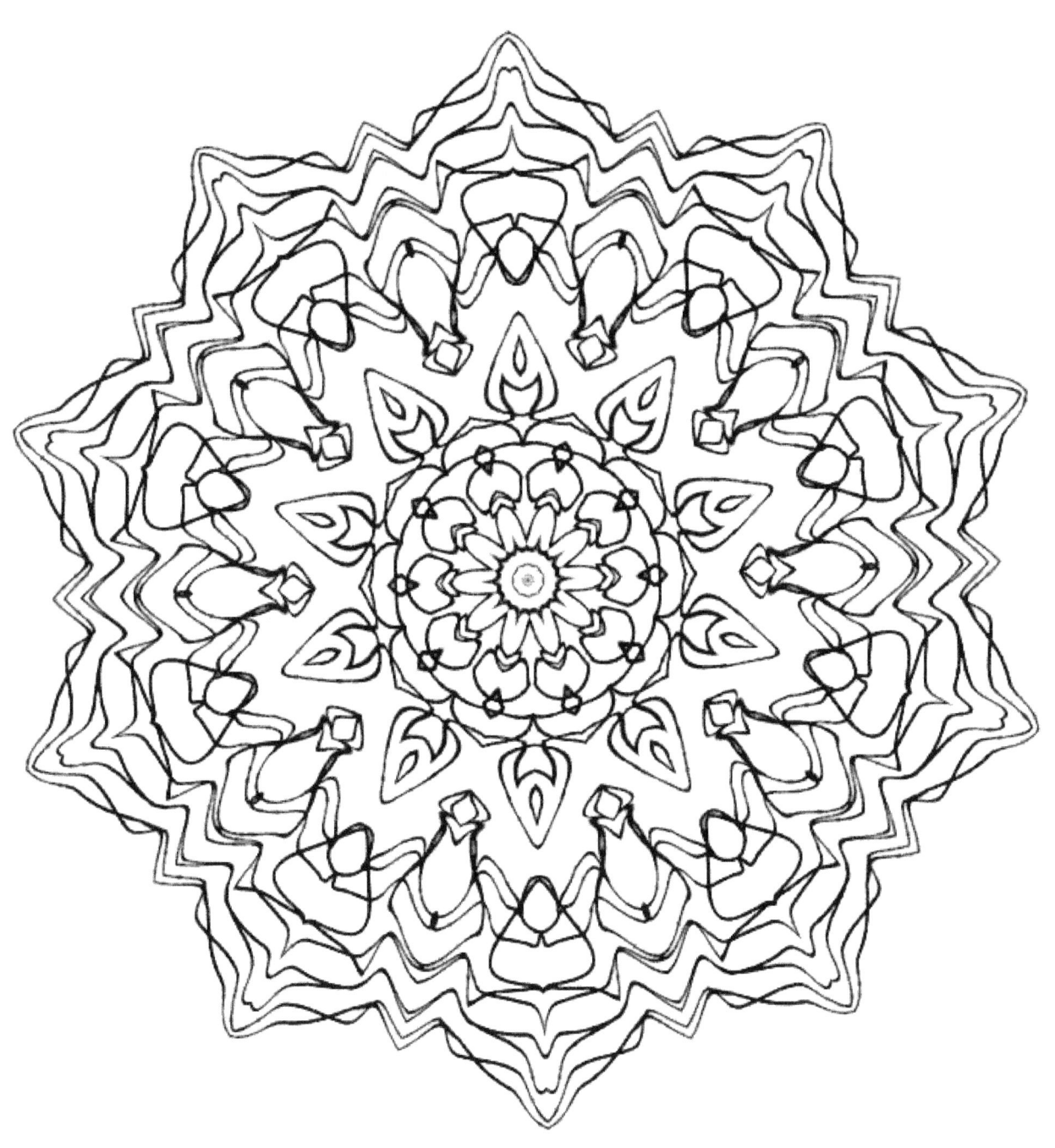

Blossom

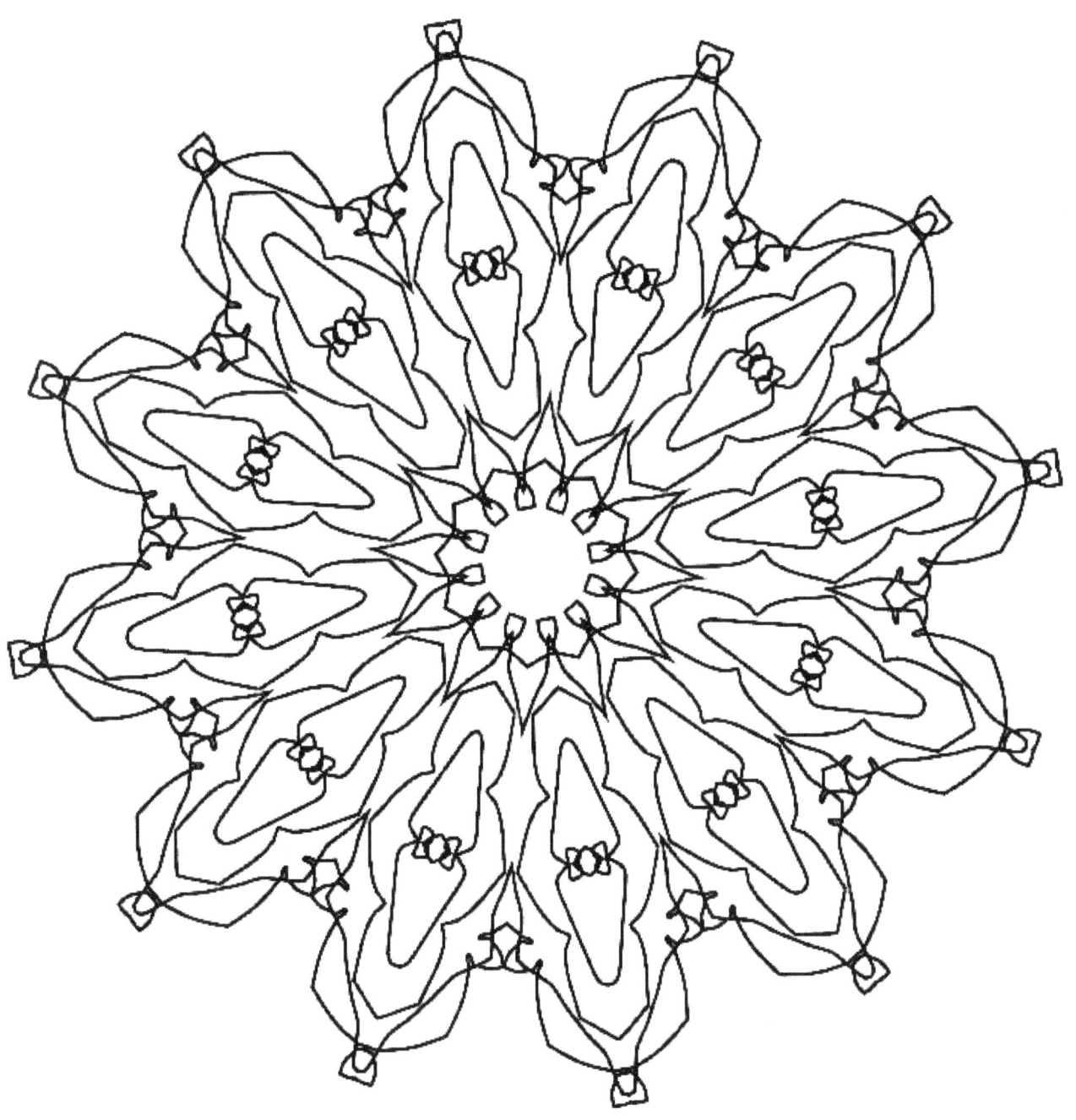

Buttons & Bows

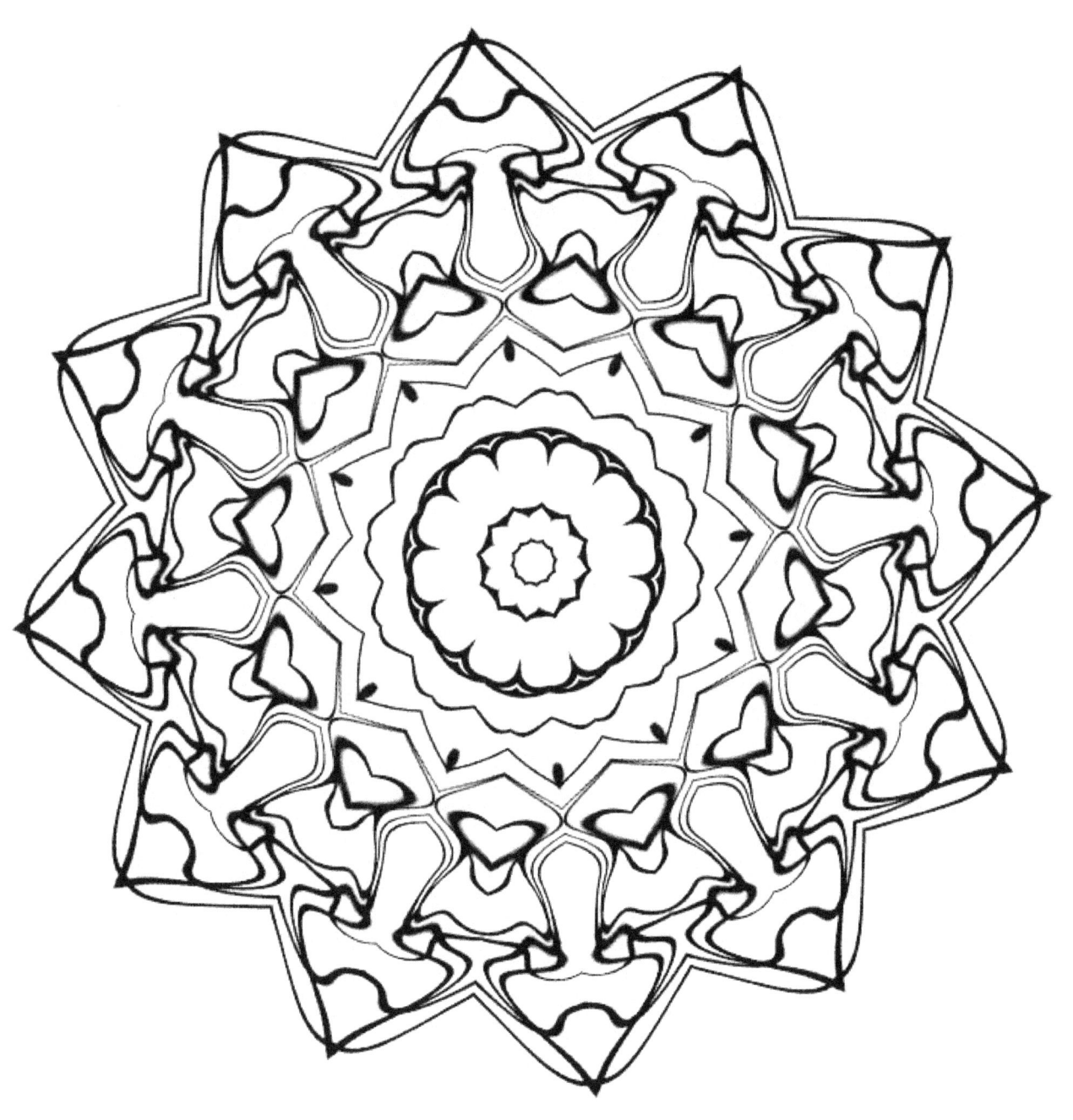

Cloisonee

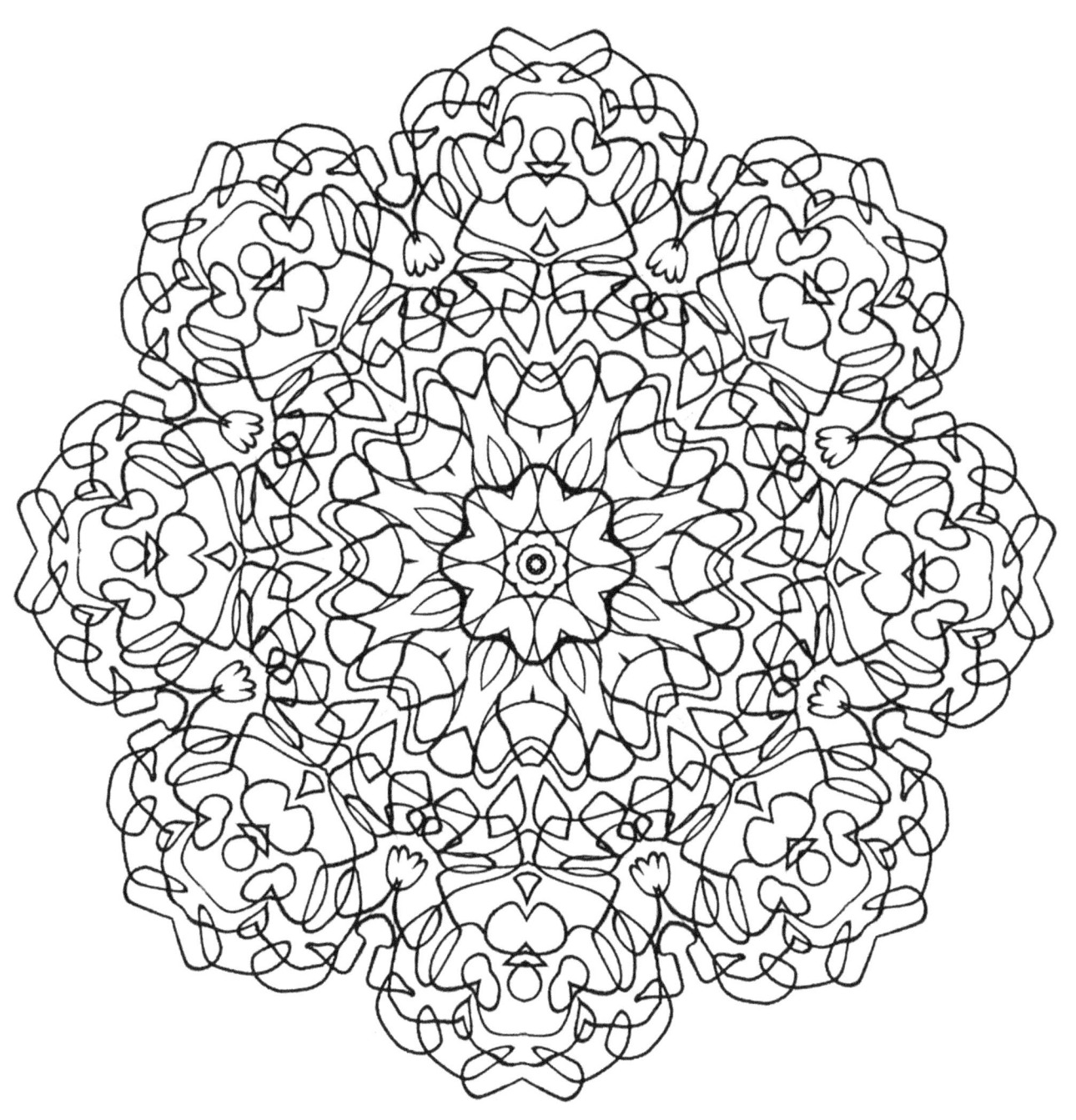

Cobblestone

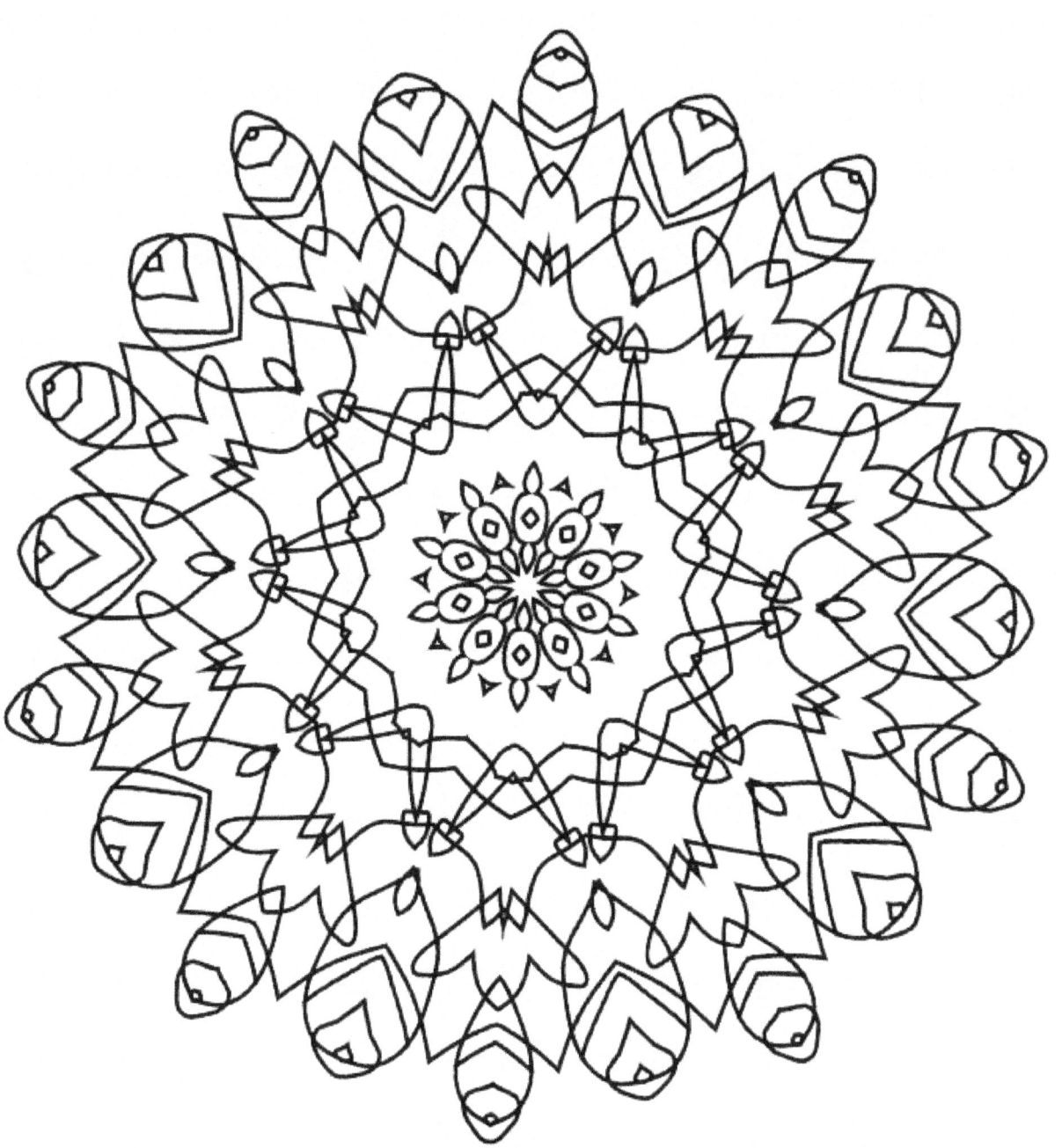

Easter

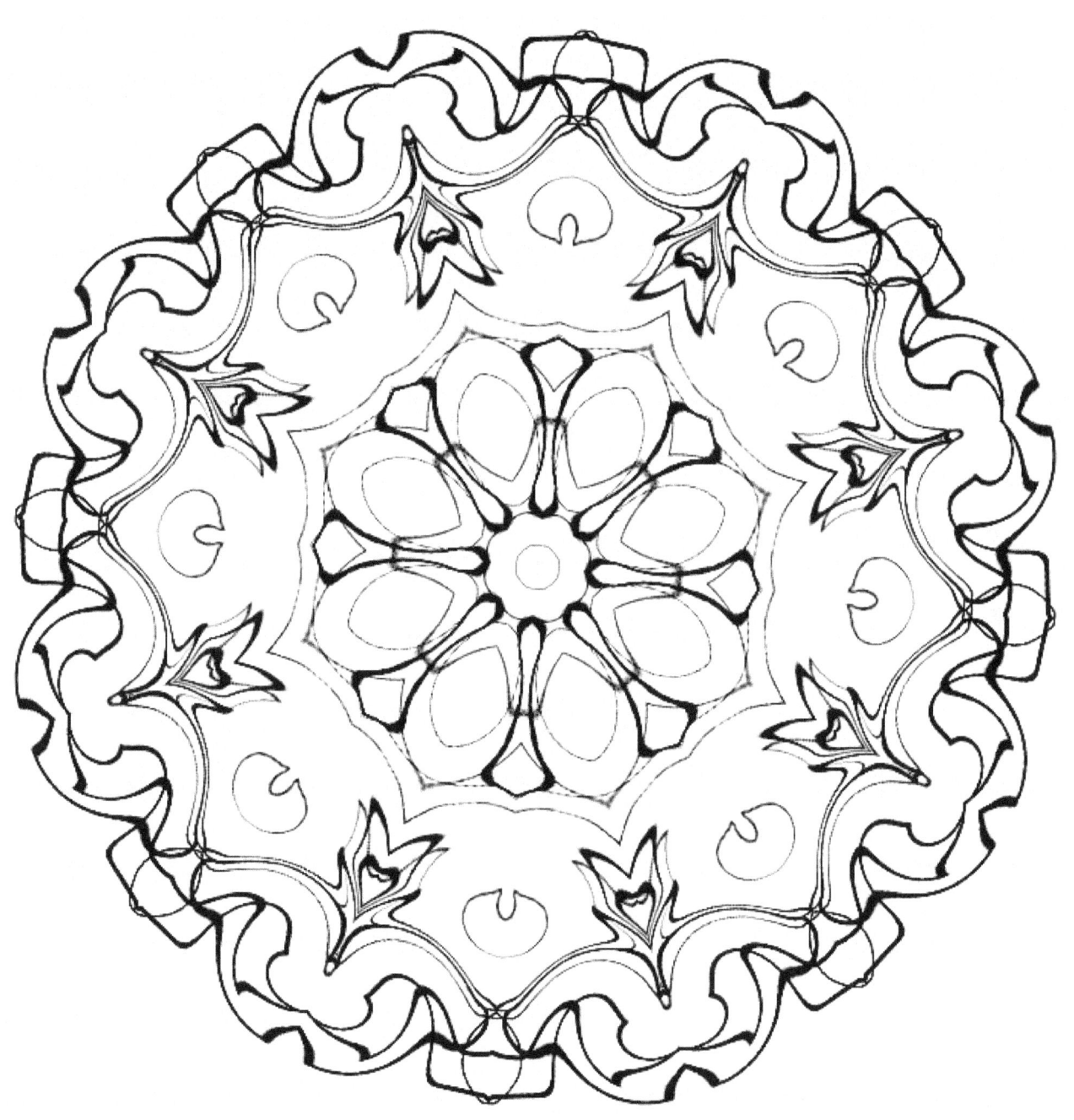

Emerging Life

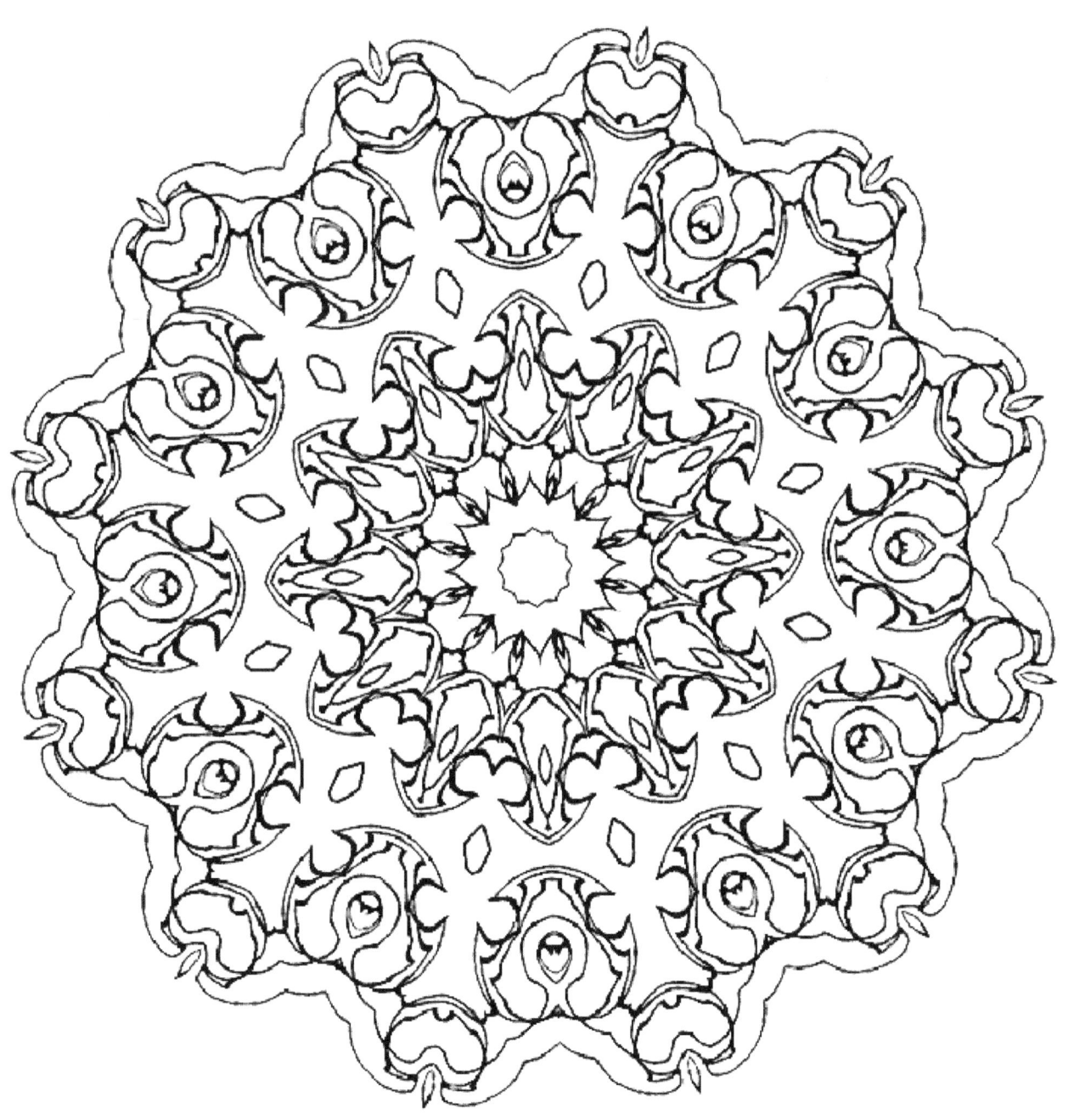

Fanciful Sundial

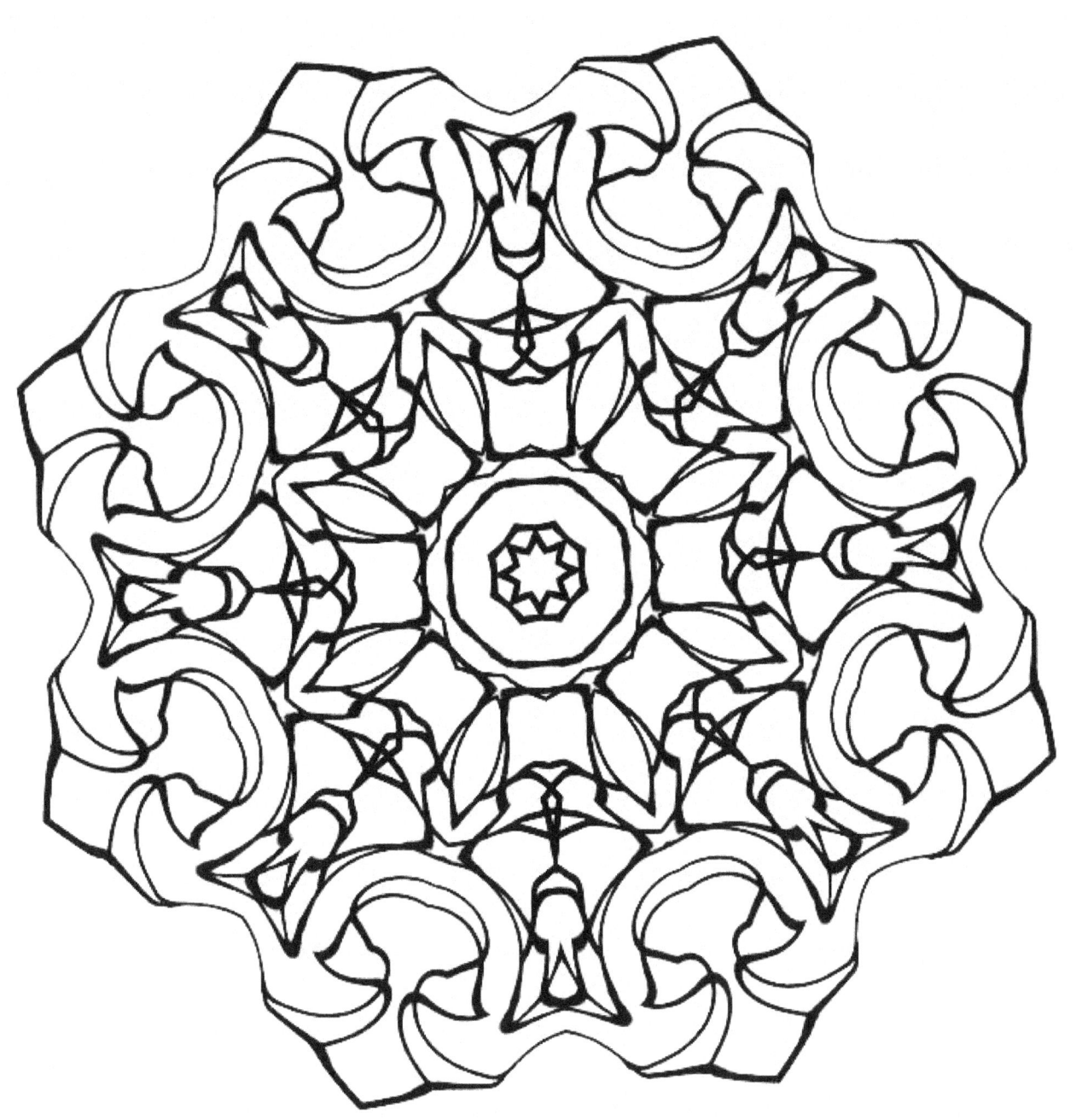

Fleur de Lis

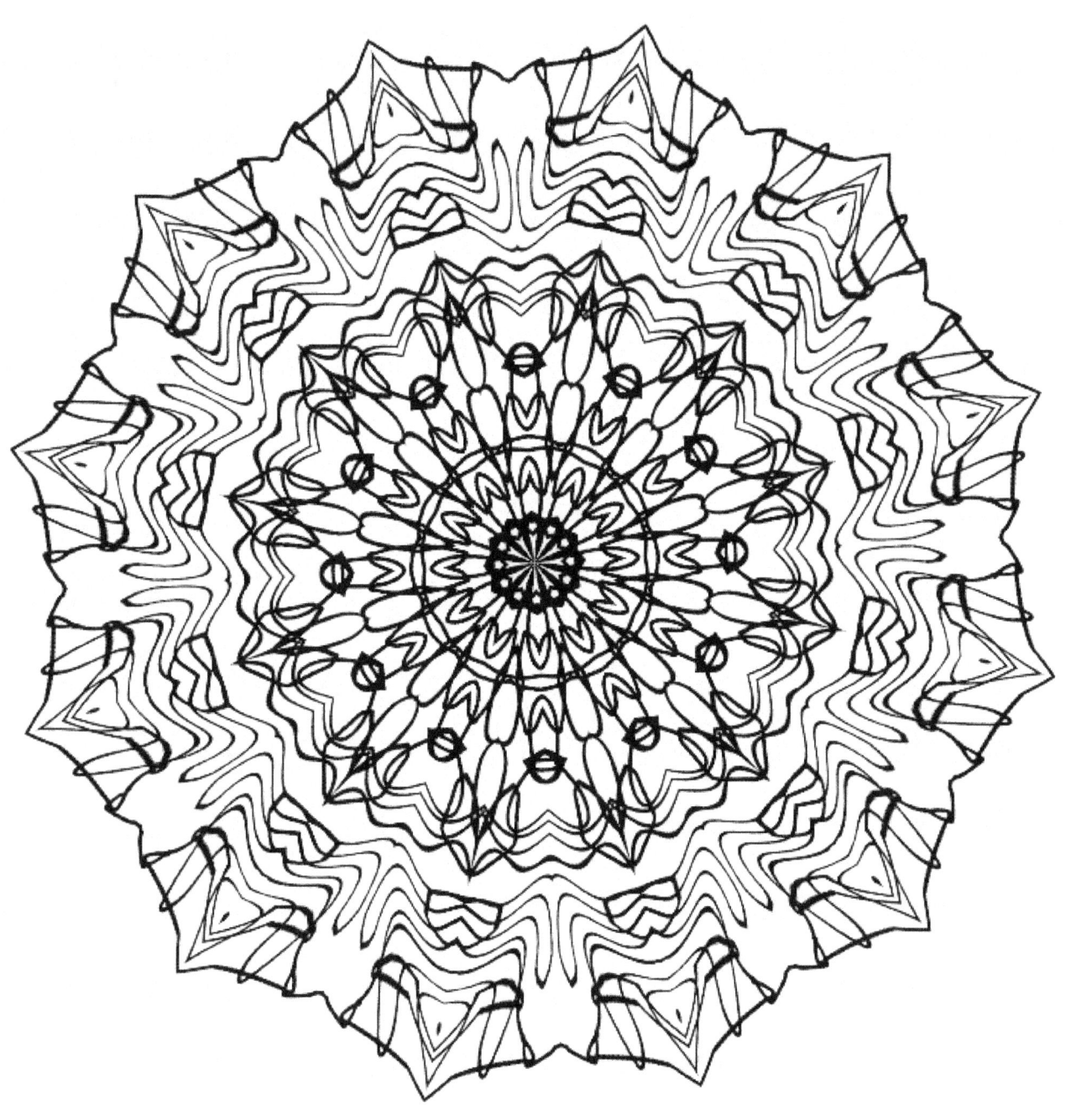

Foolish

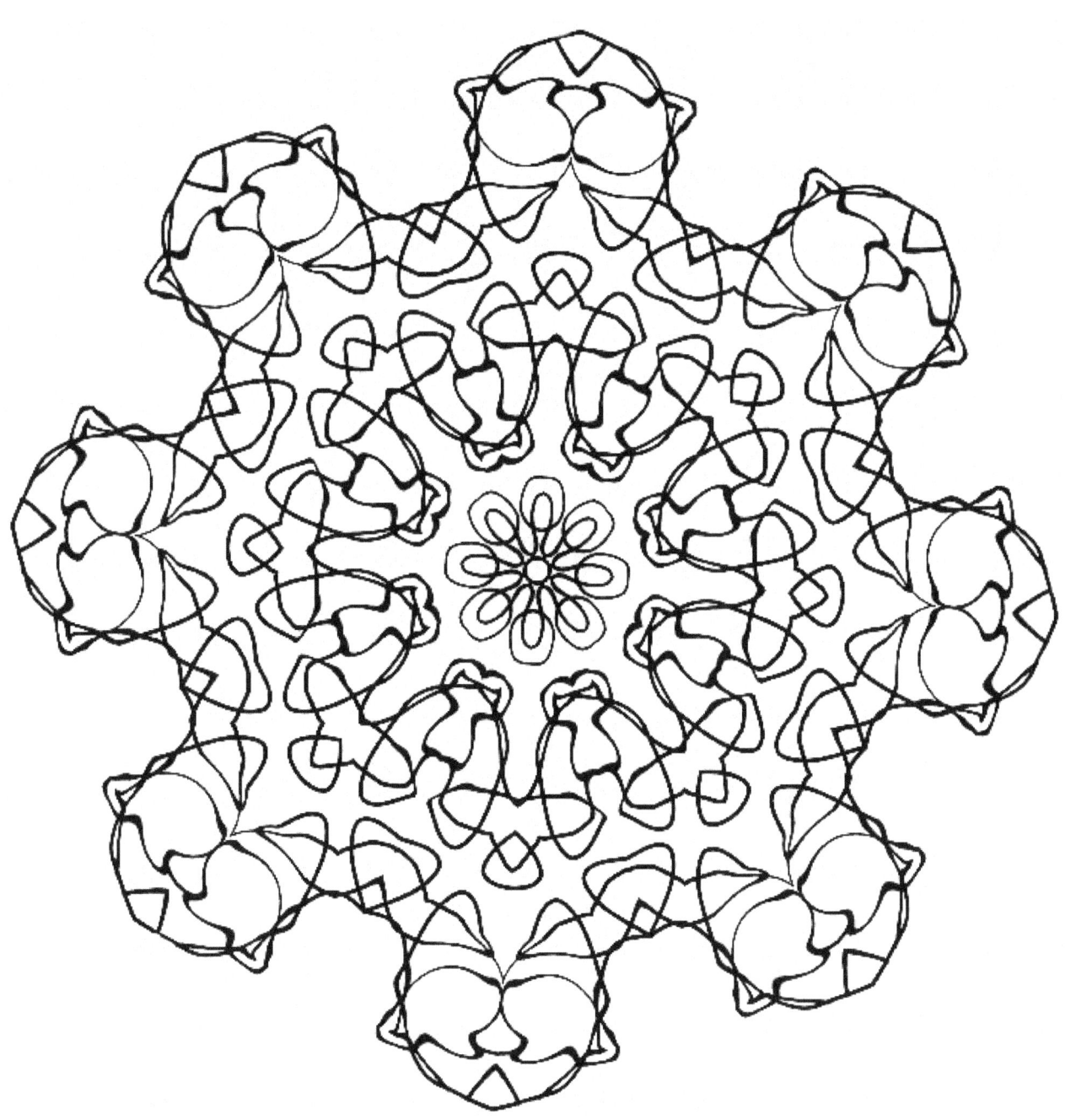

Fortune

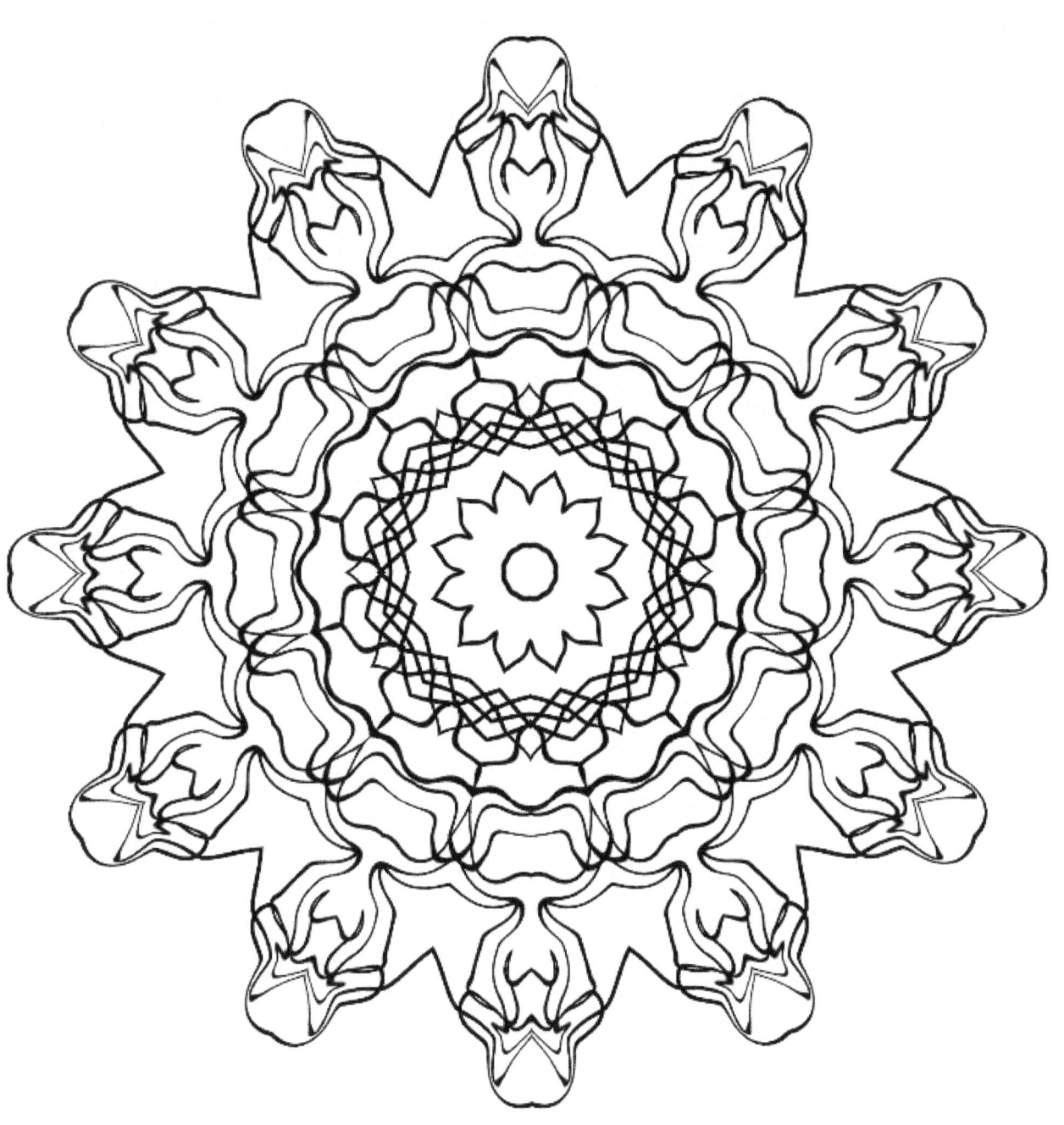

Grinch

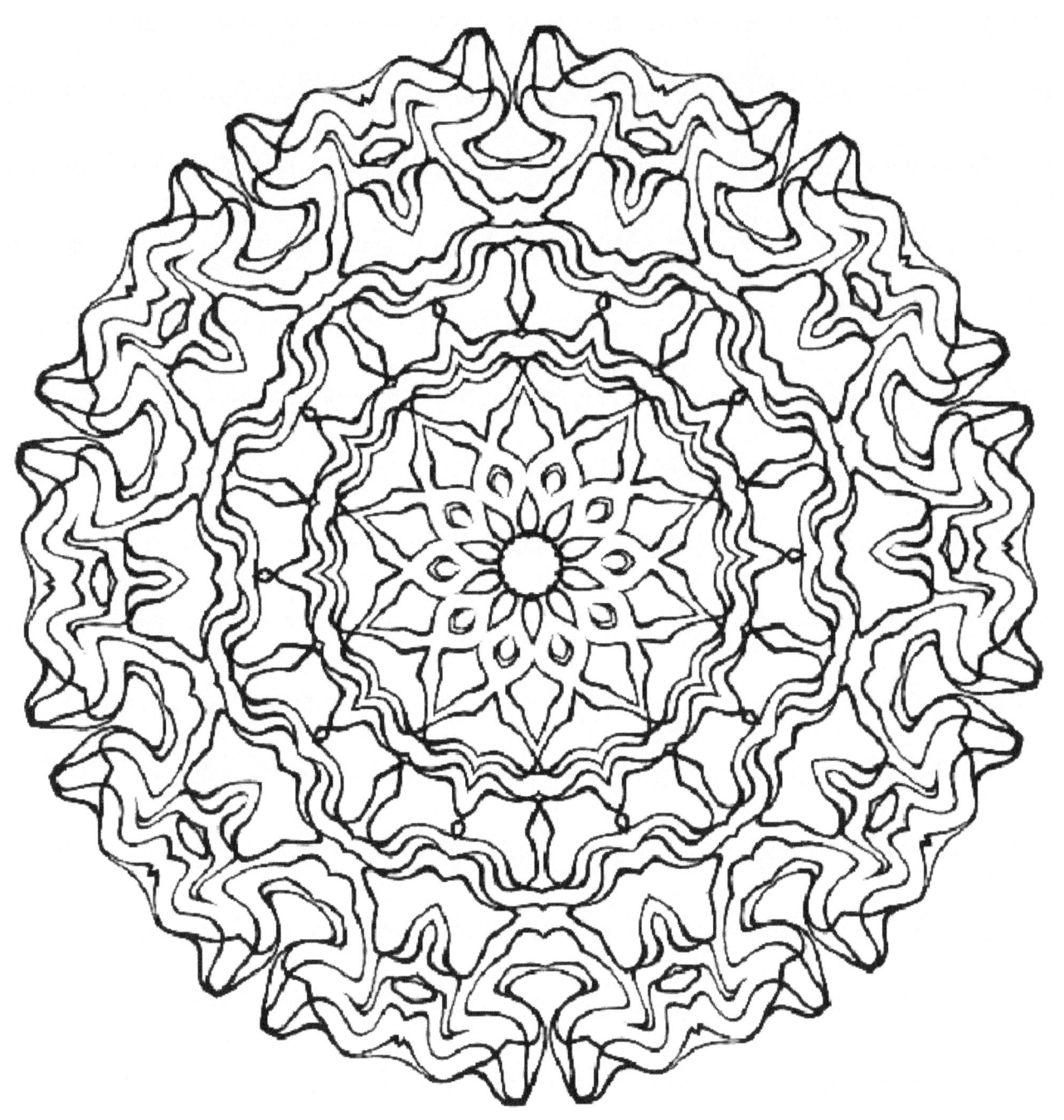

Happy

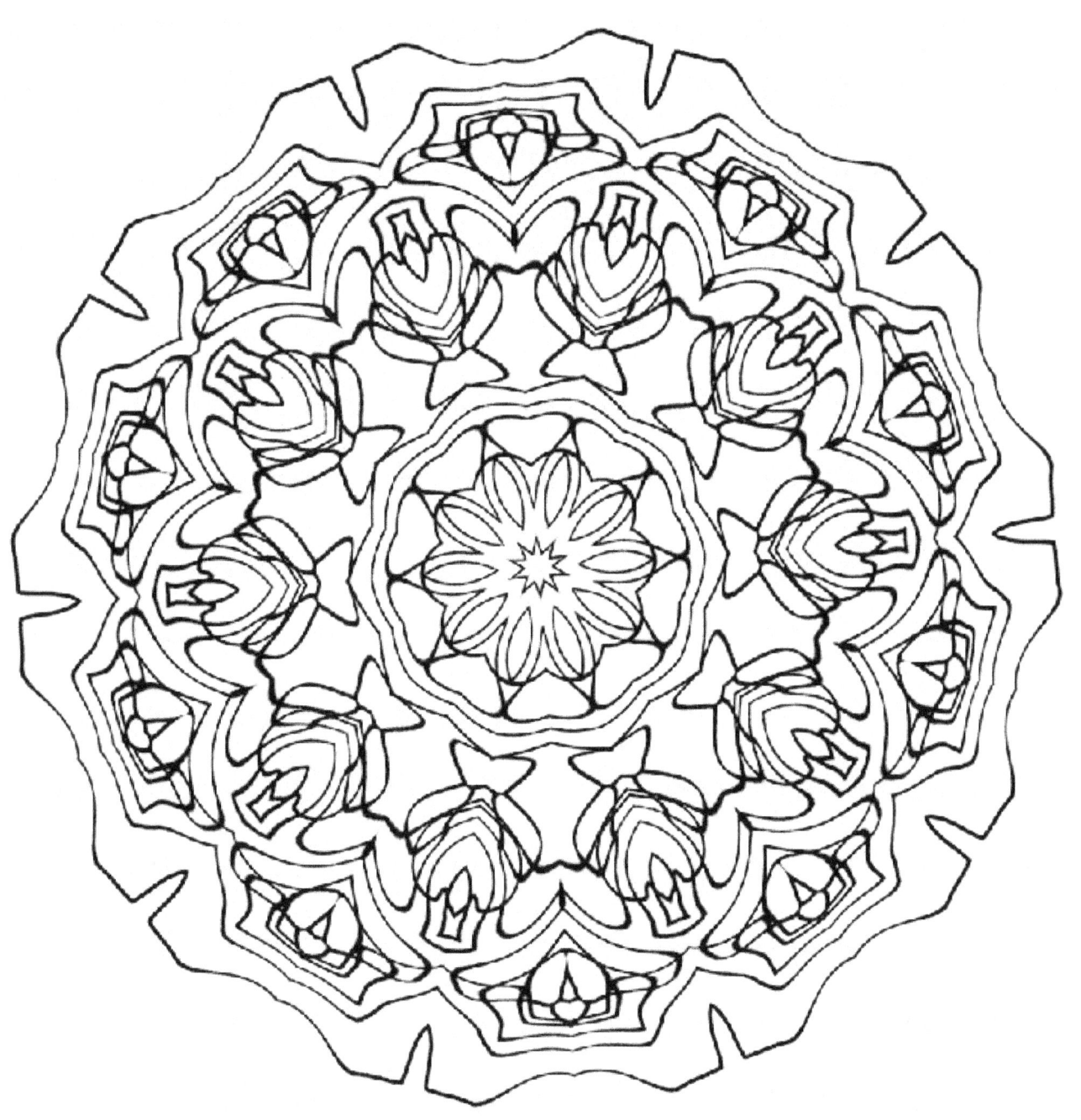

Harvest

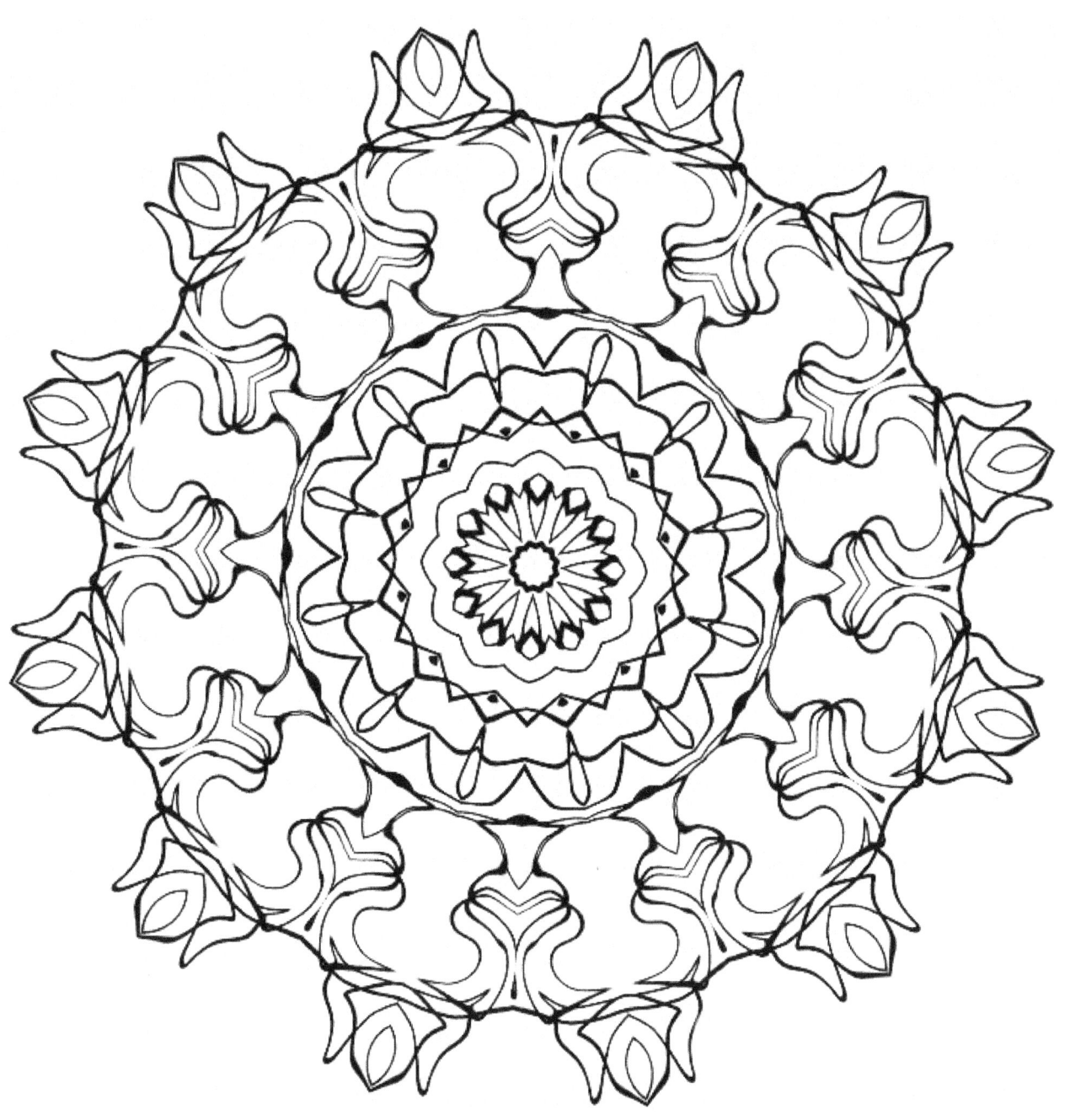

Hearts & Spades

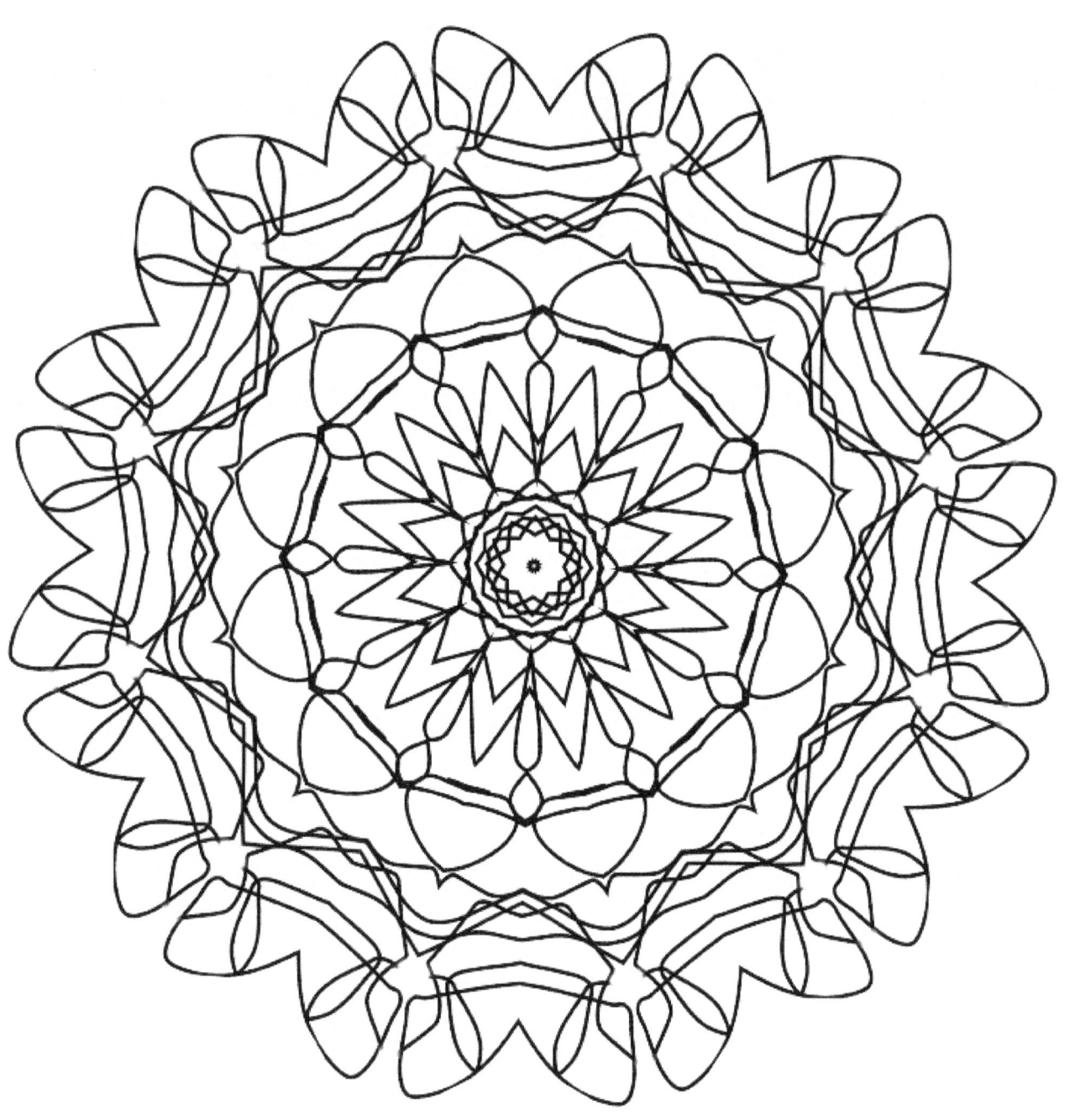

Inversion

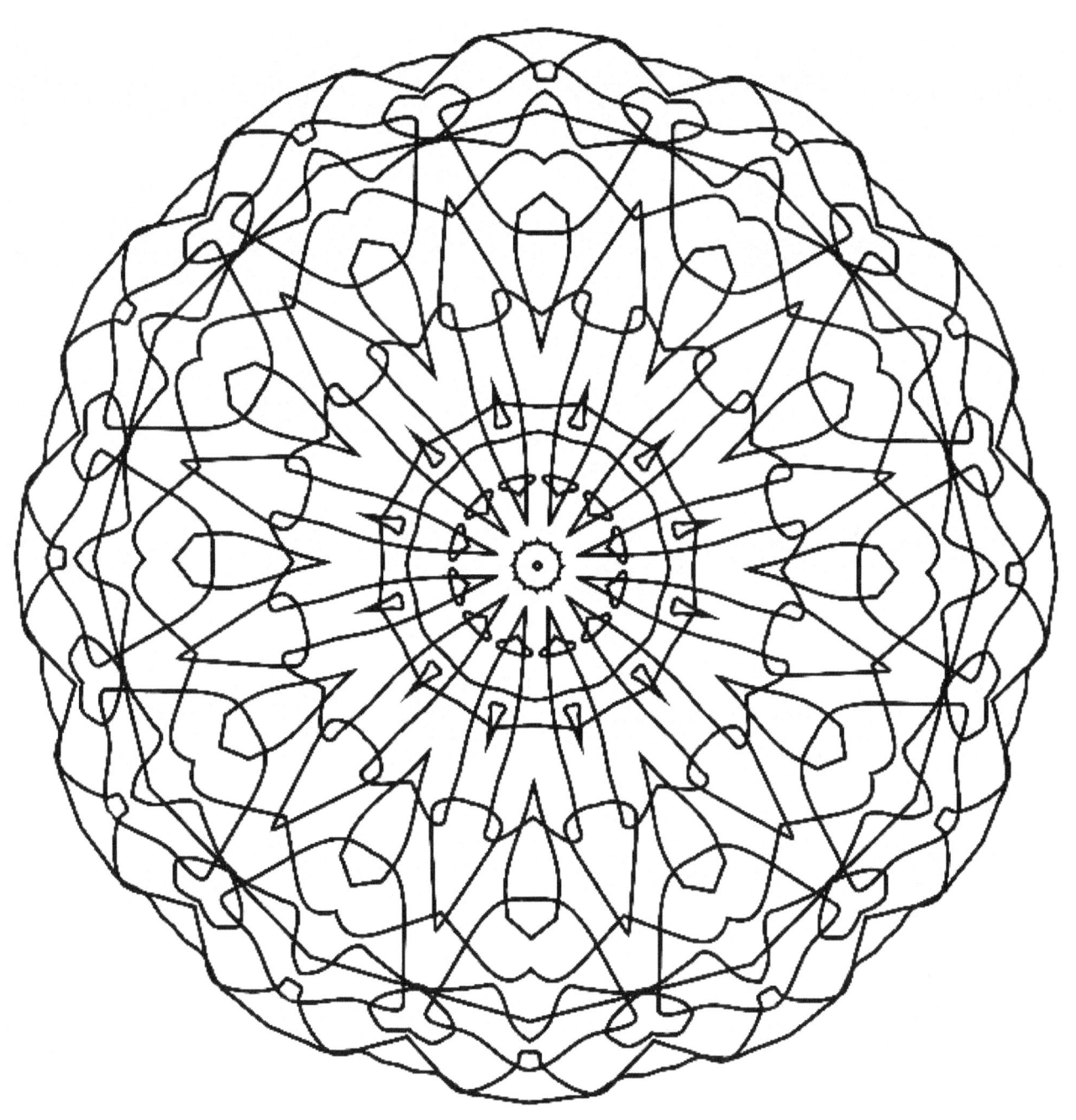

Jewel Inlay

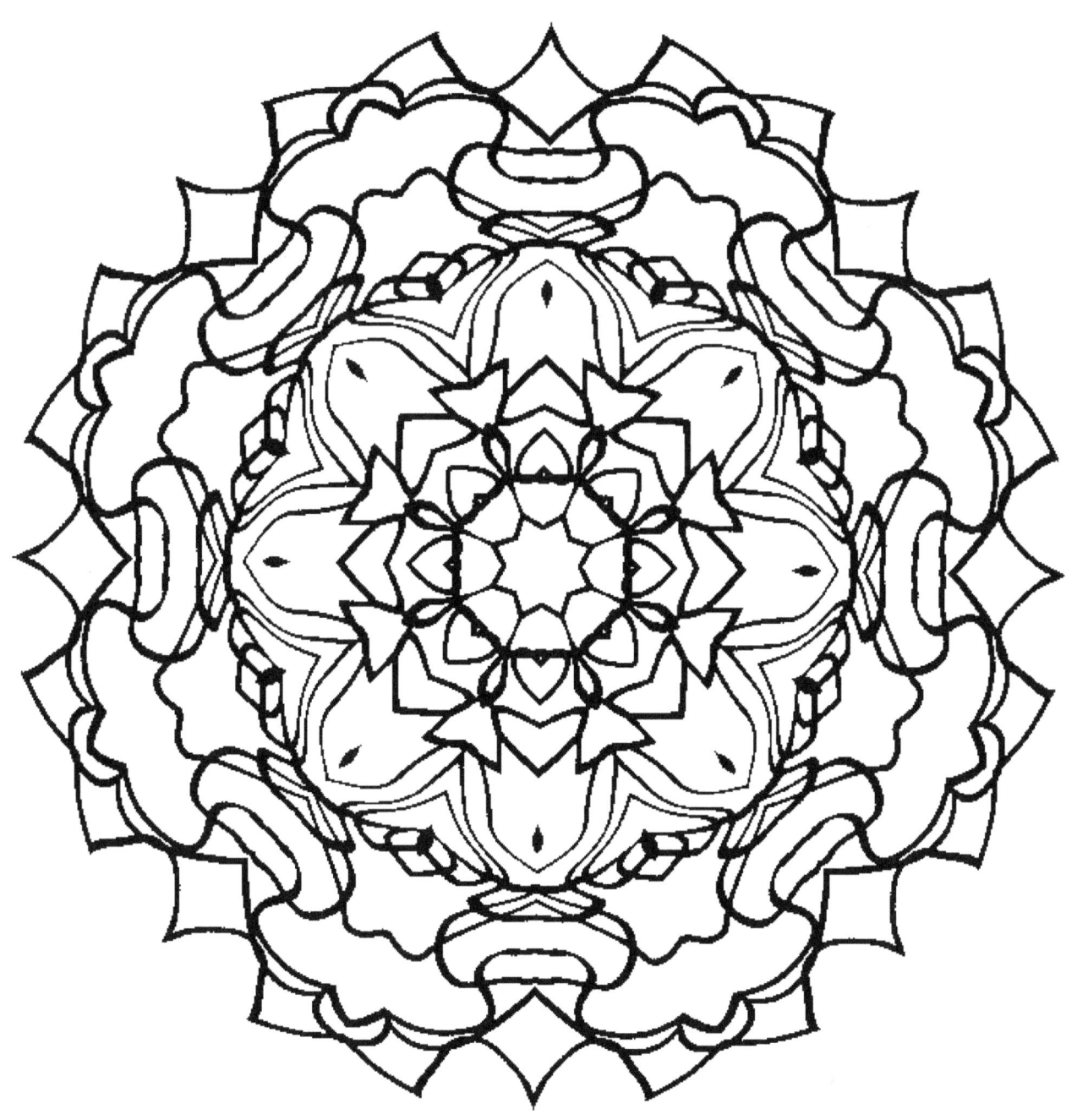

Jungle Flower

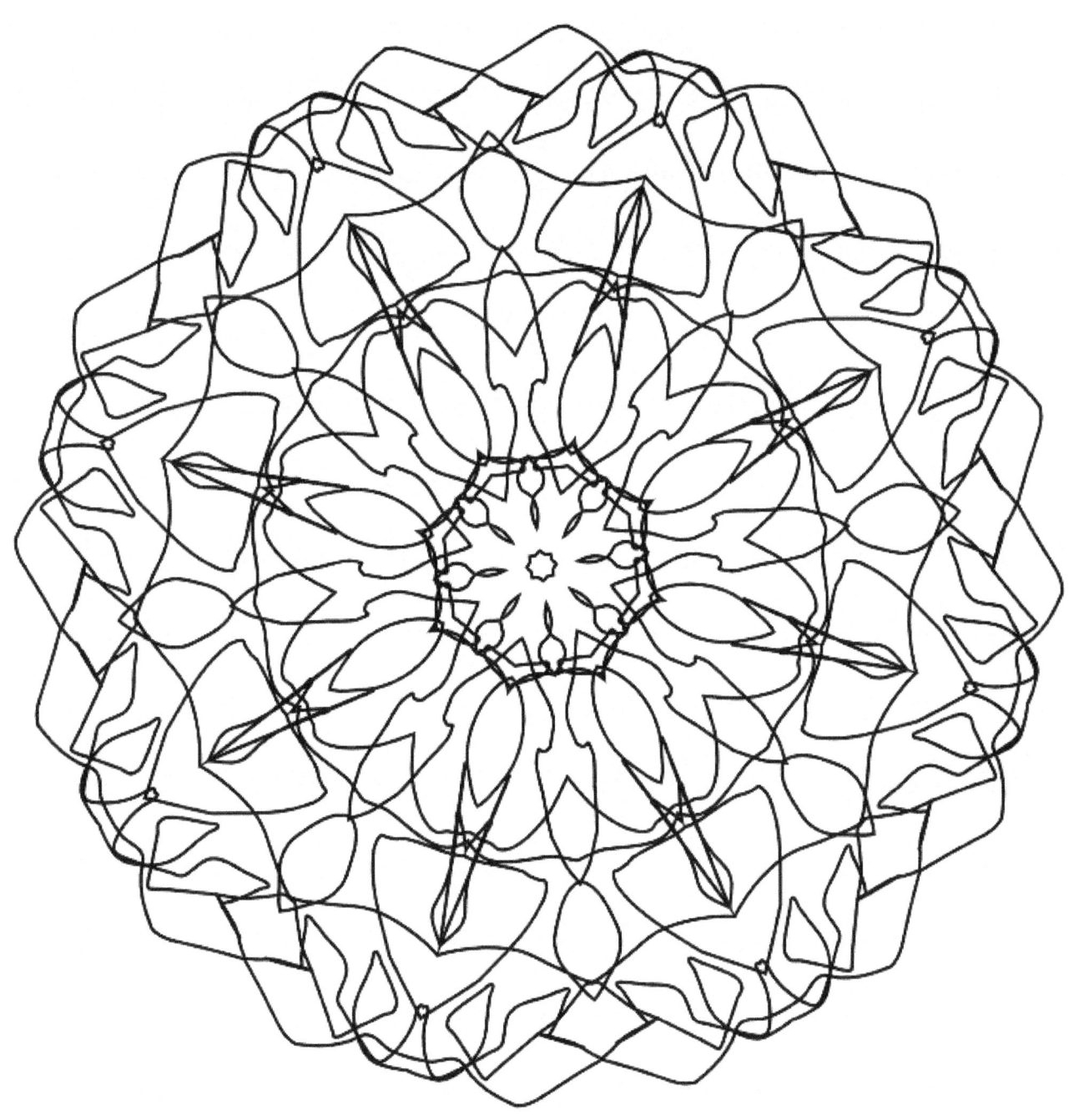

Jungle Hunter

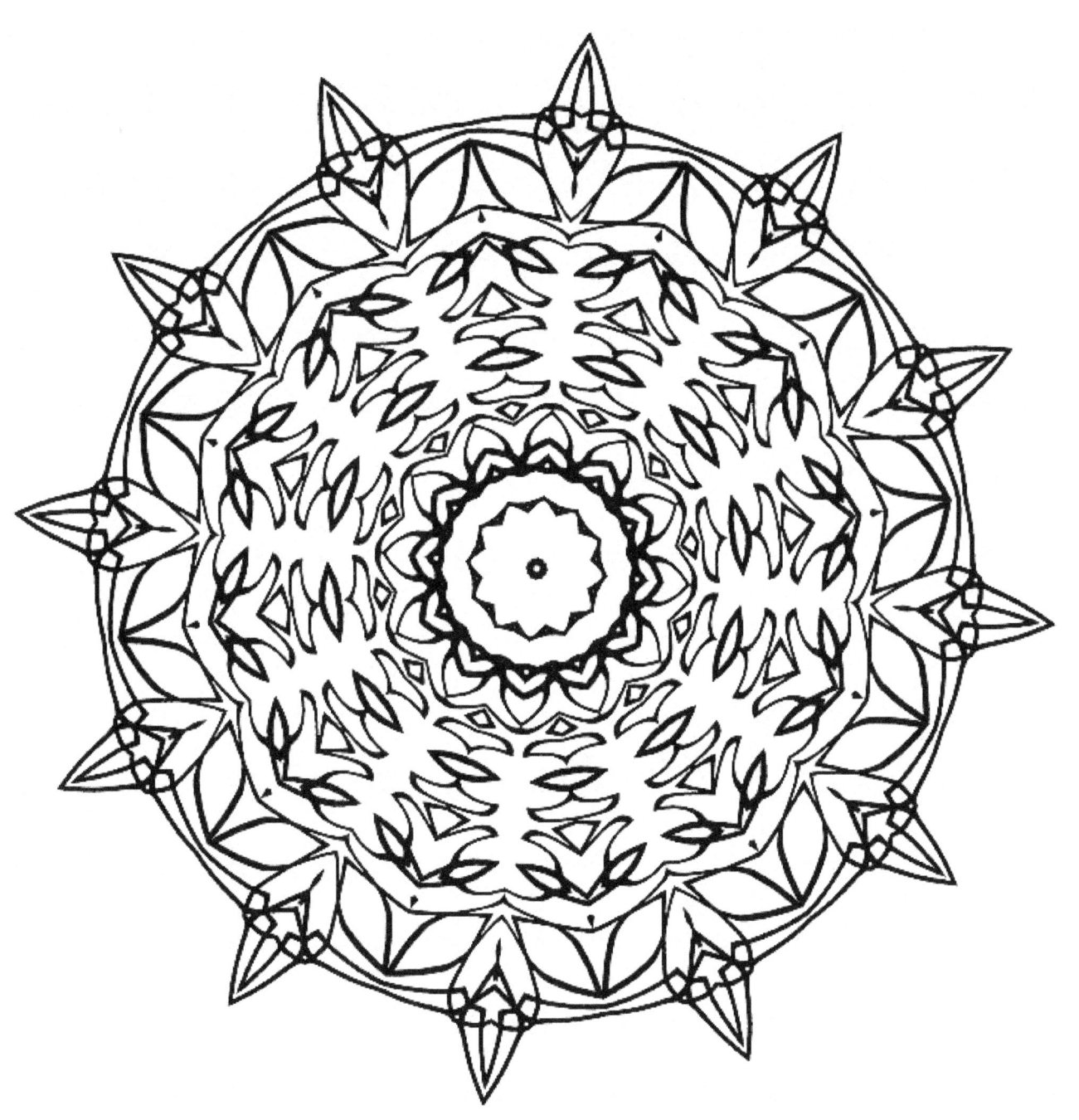

Lily Pond

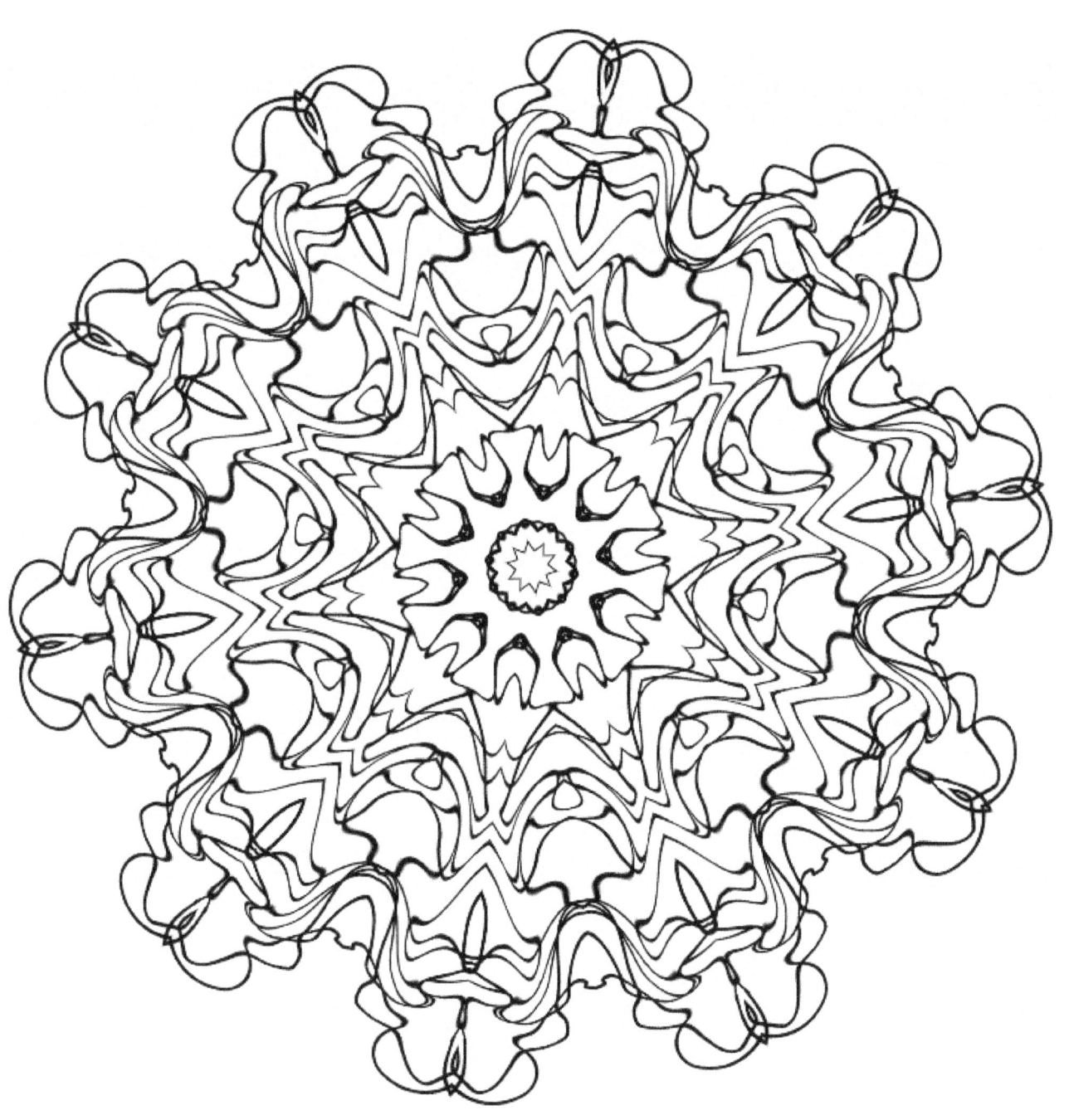

Needle's Eye

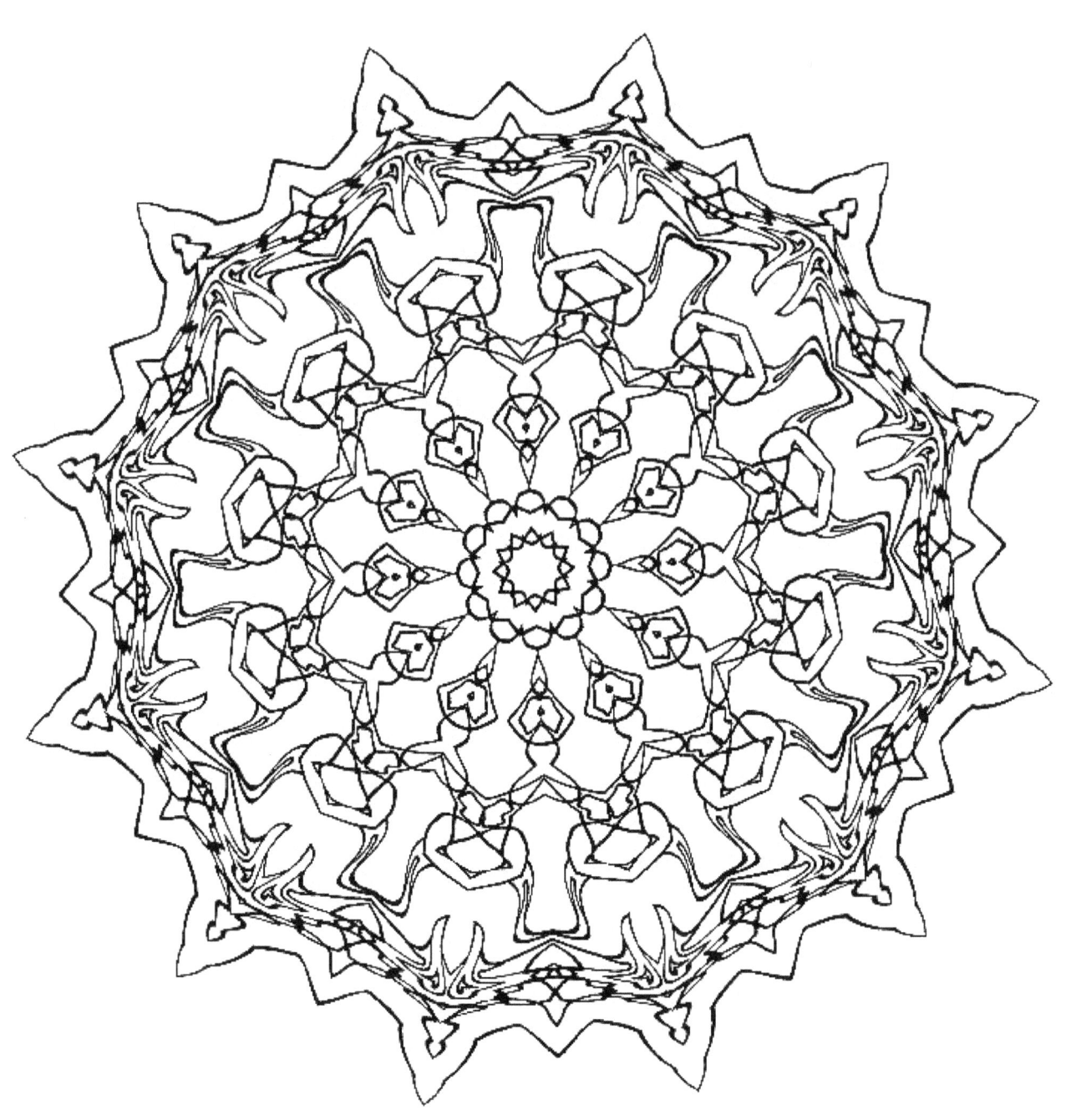

Neptune Clock

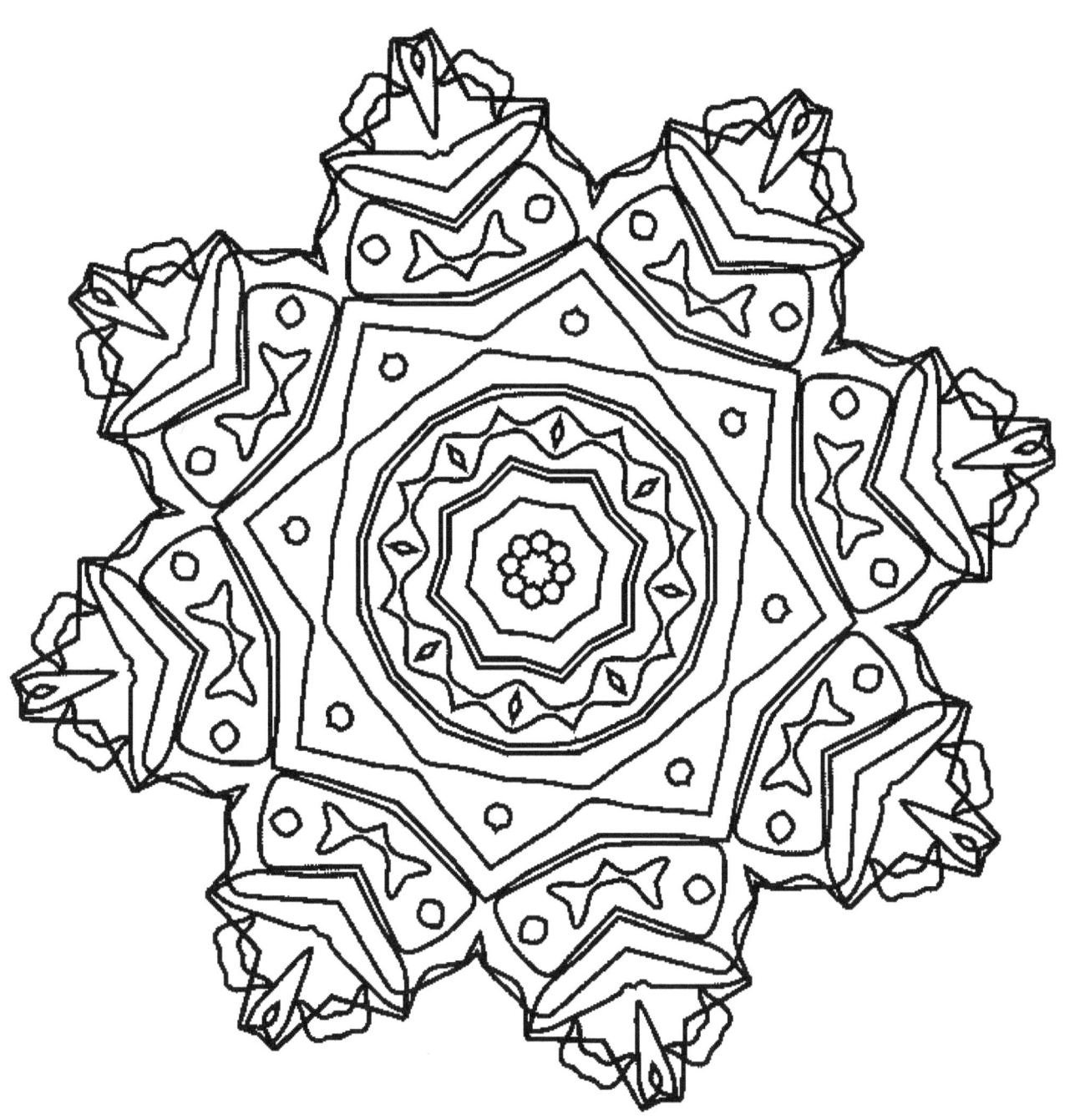

Ornate Stoppers

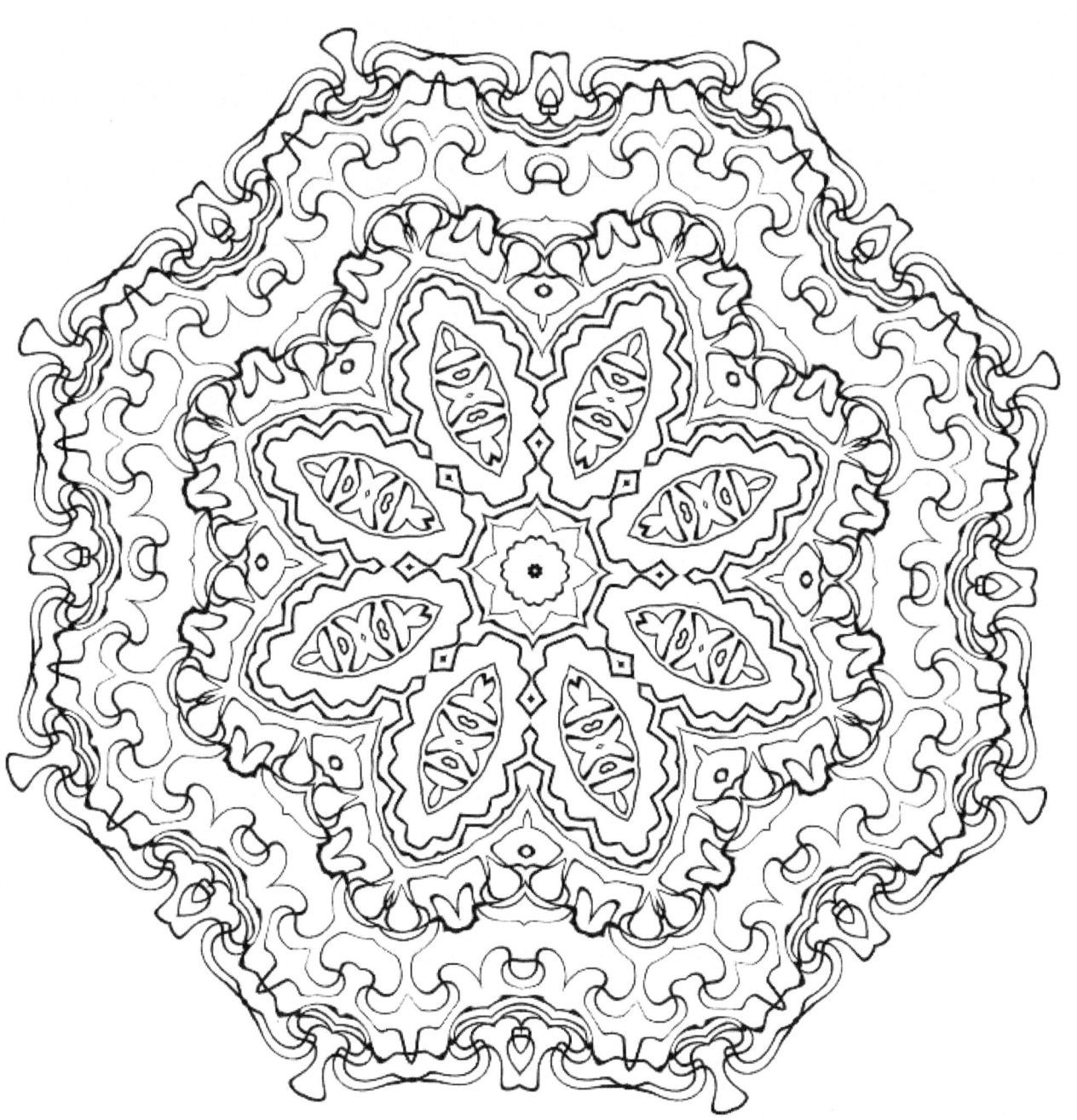

Pysanky

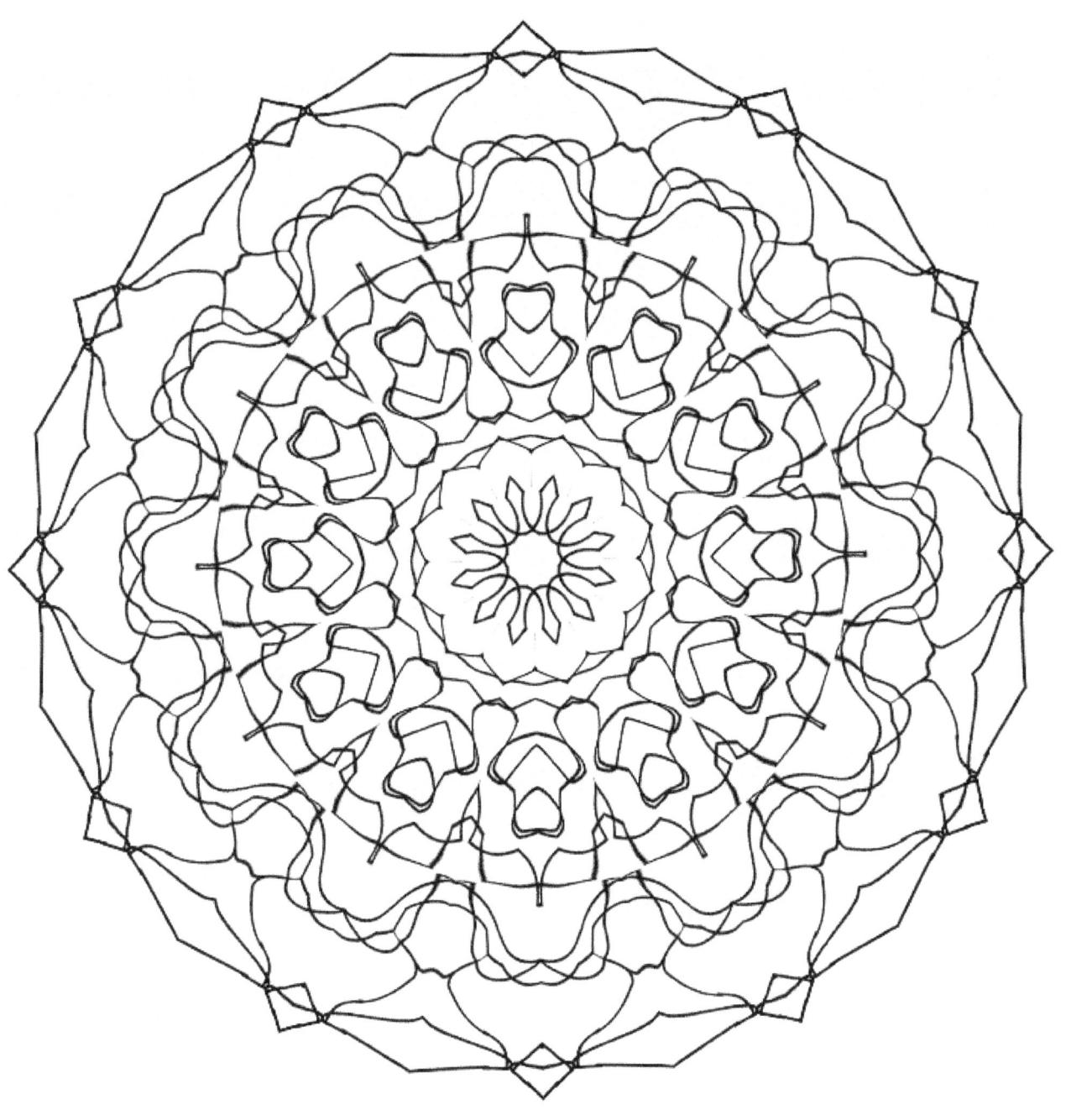

Queen of Hearts

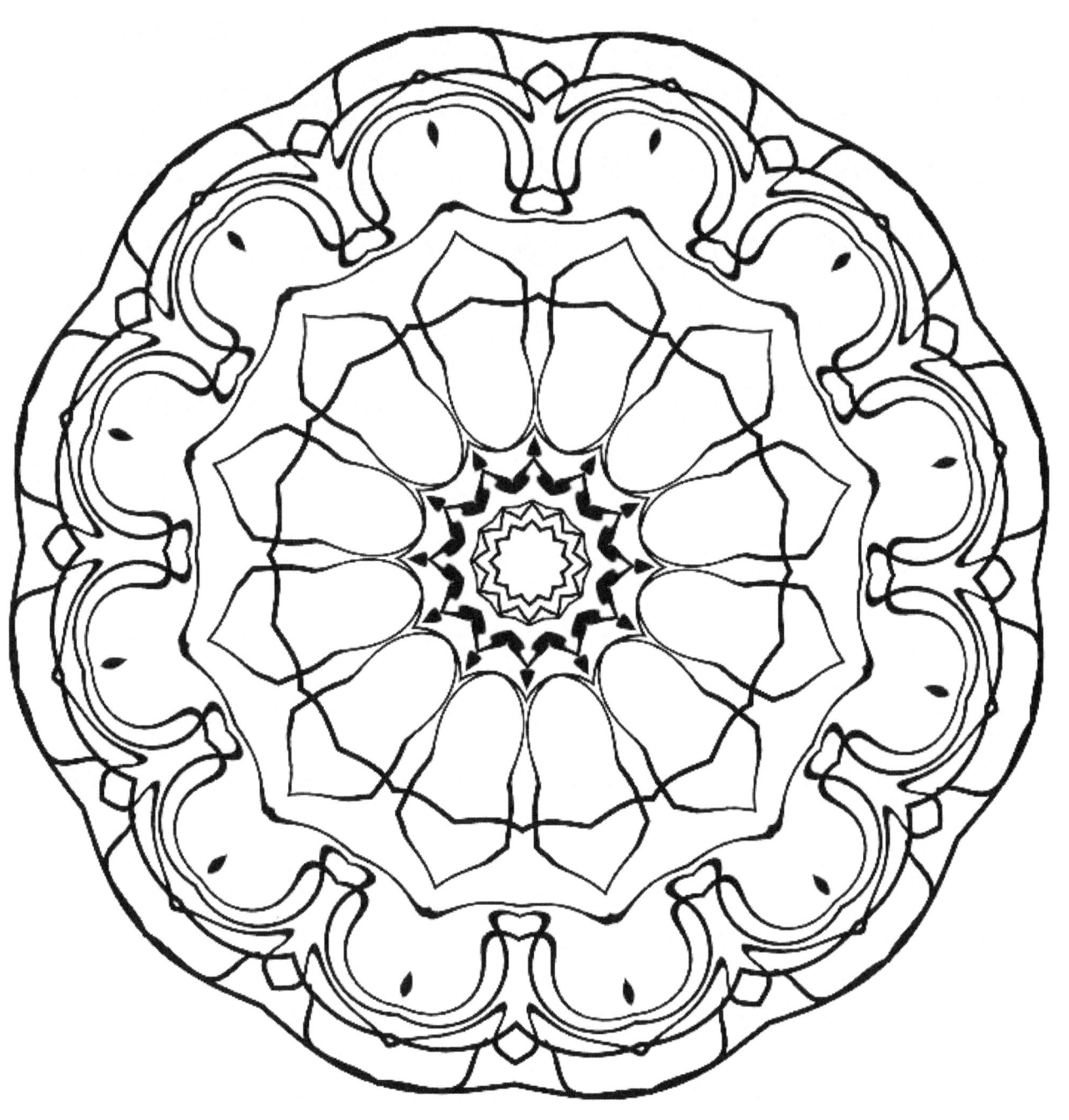

Stained Glass Porthole

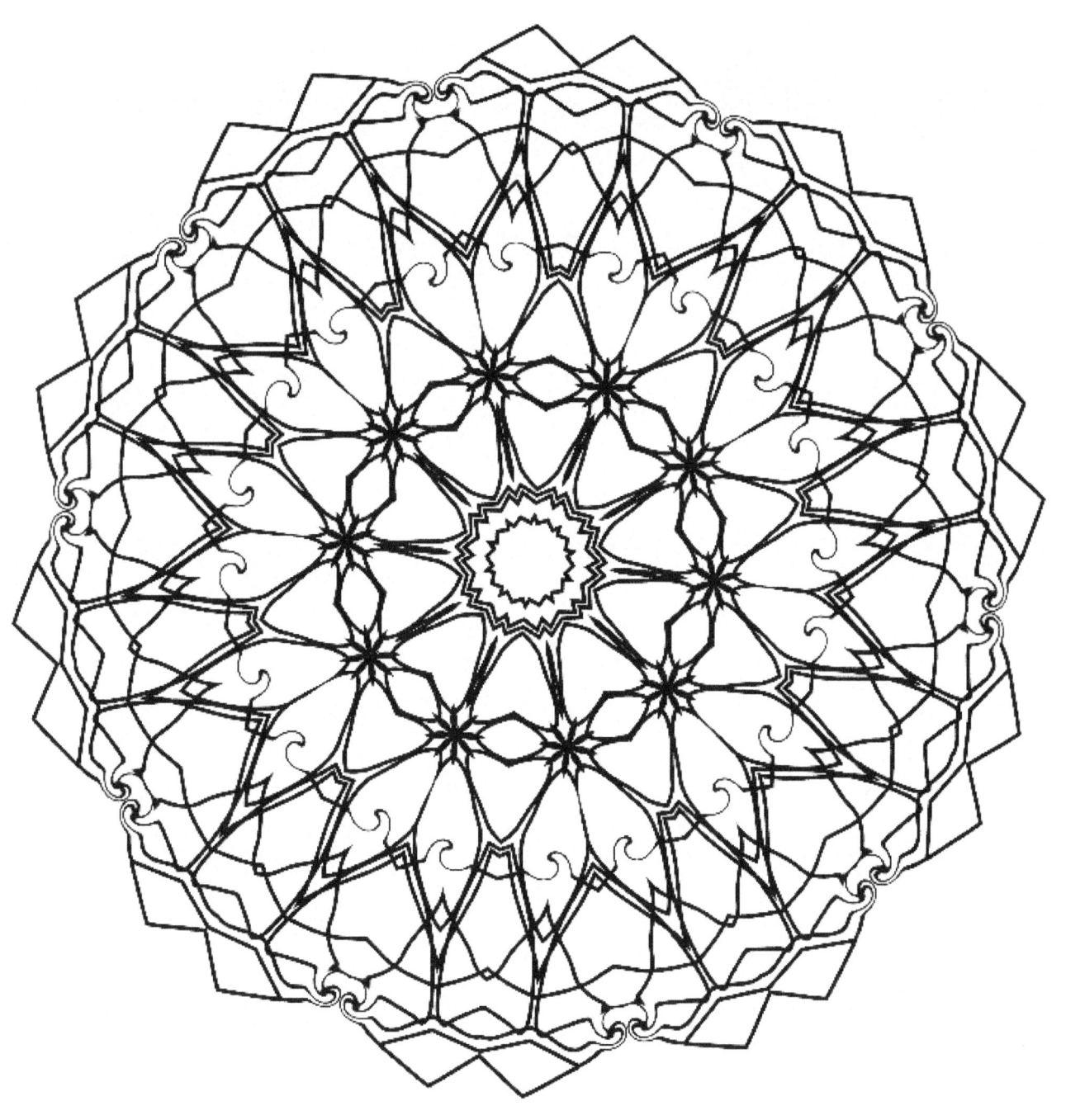

Sunshine & Flowers

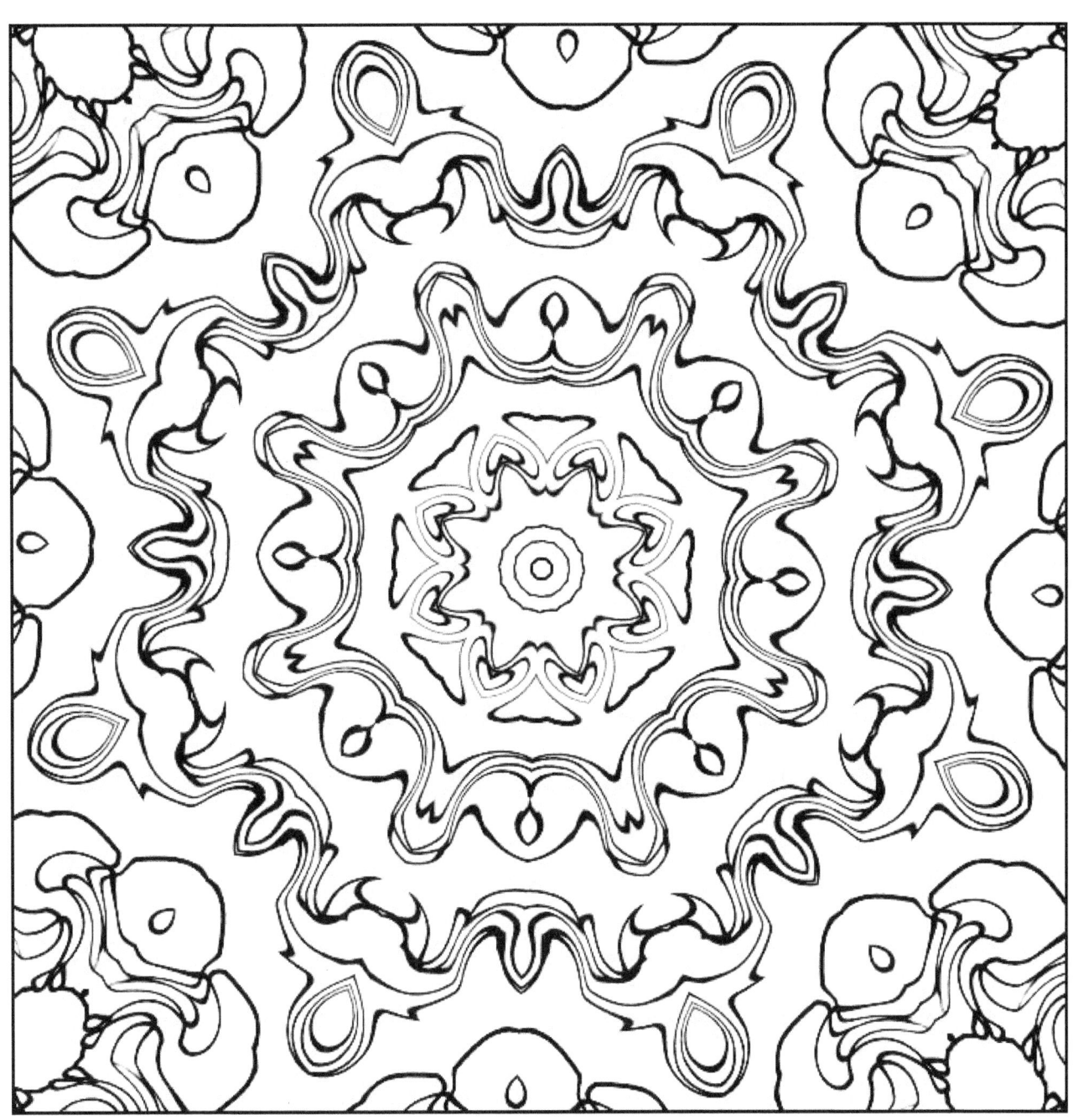

Swirls & Curls

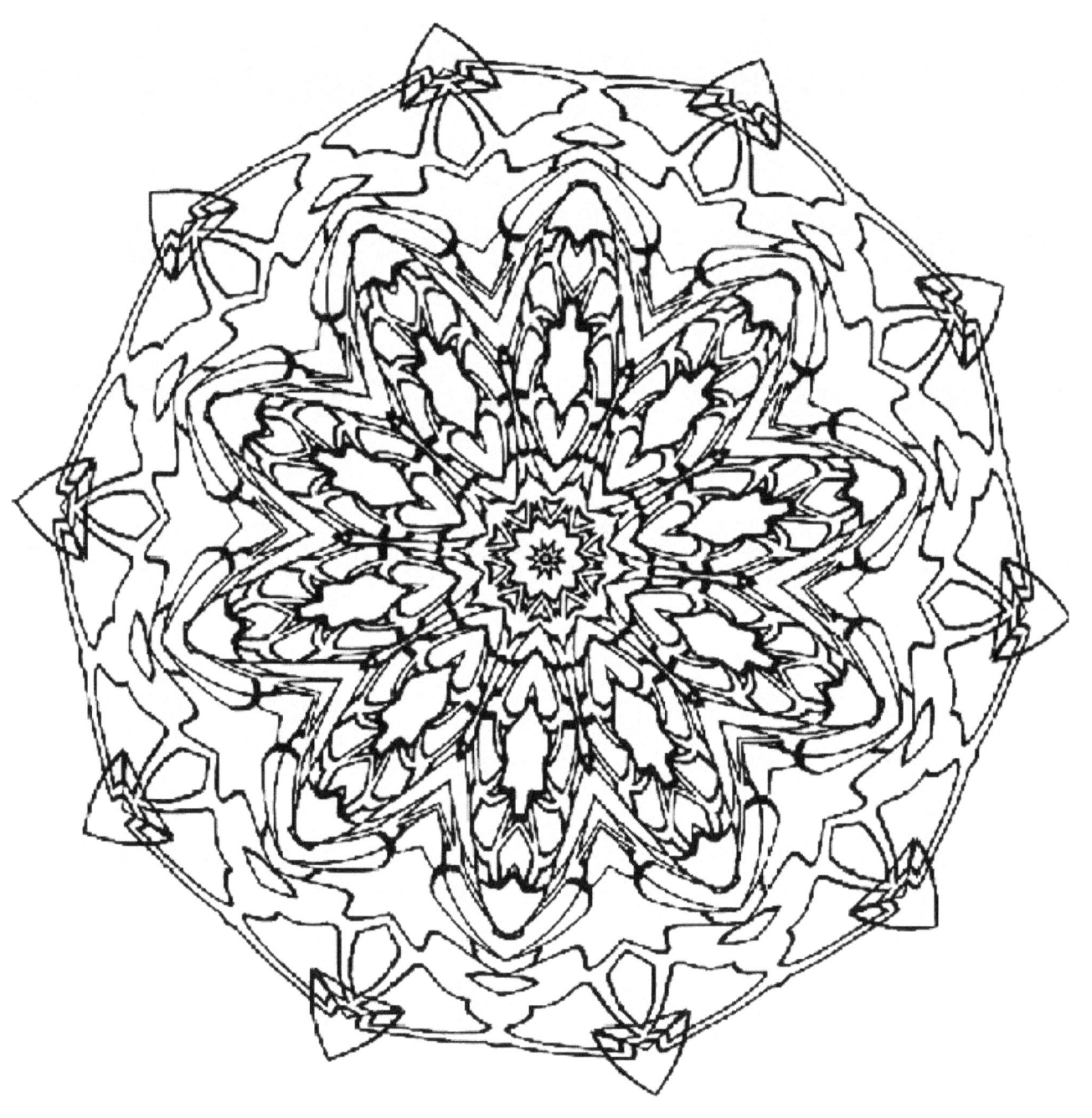

Tangled

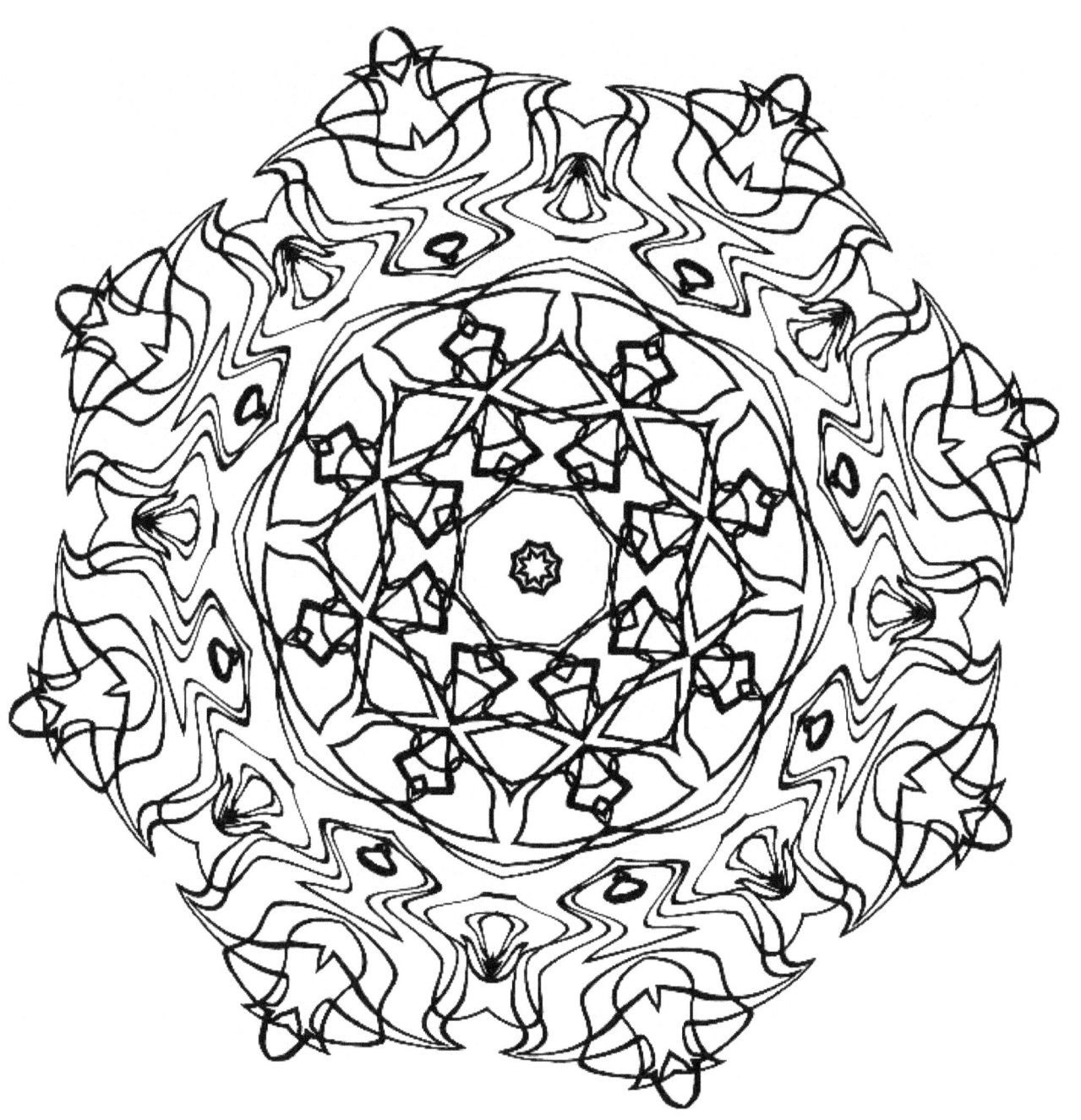

Tile Inlay

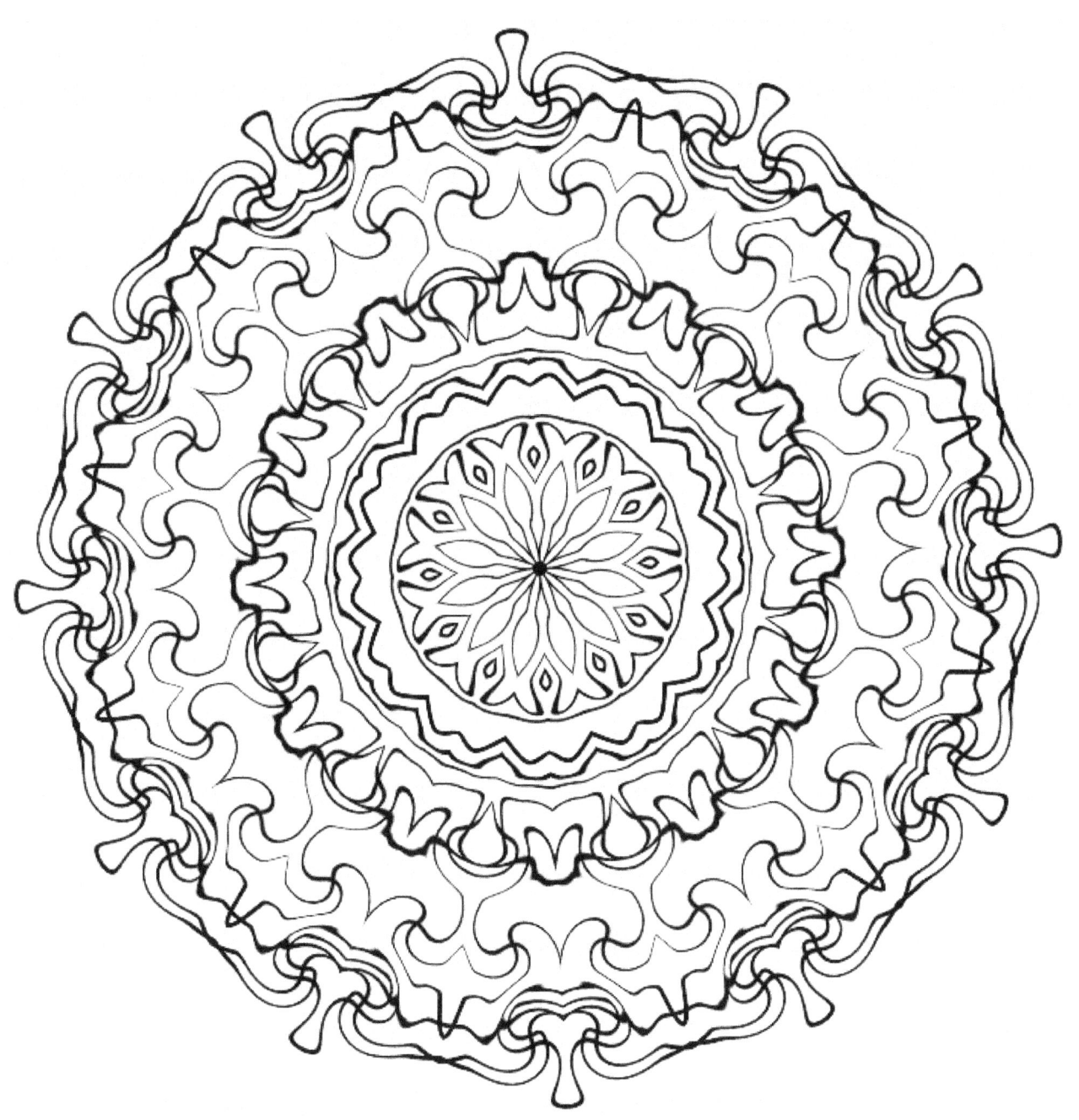

Tiled Fountain

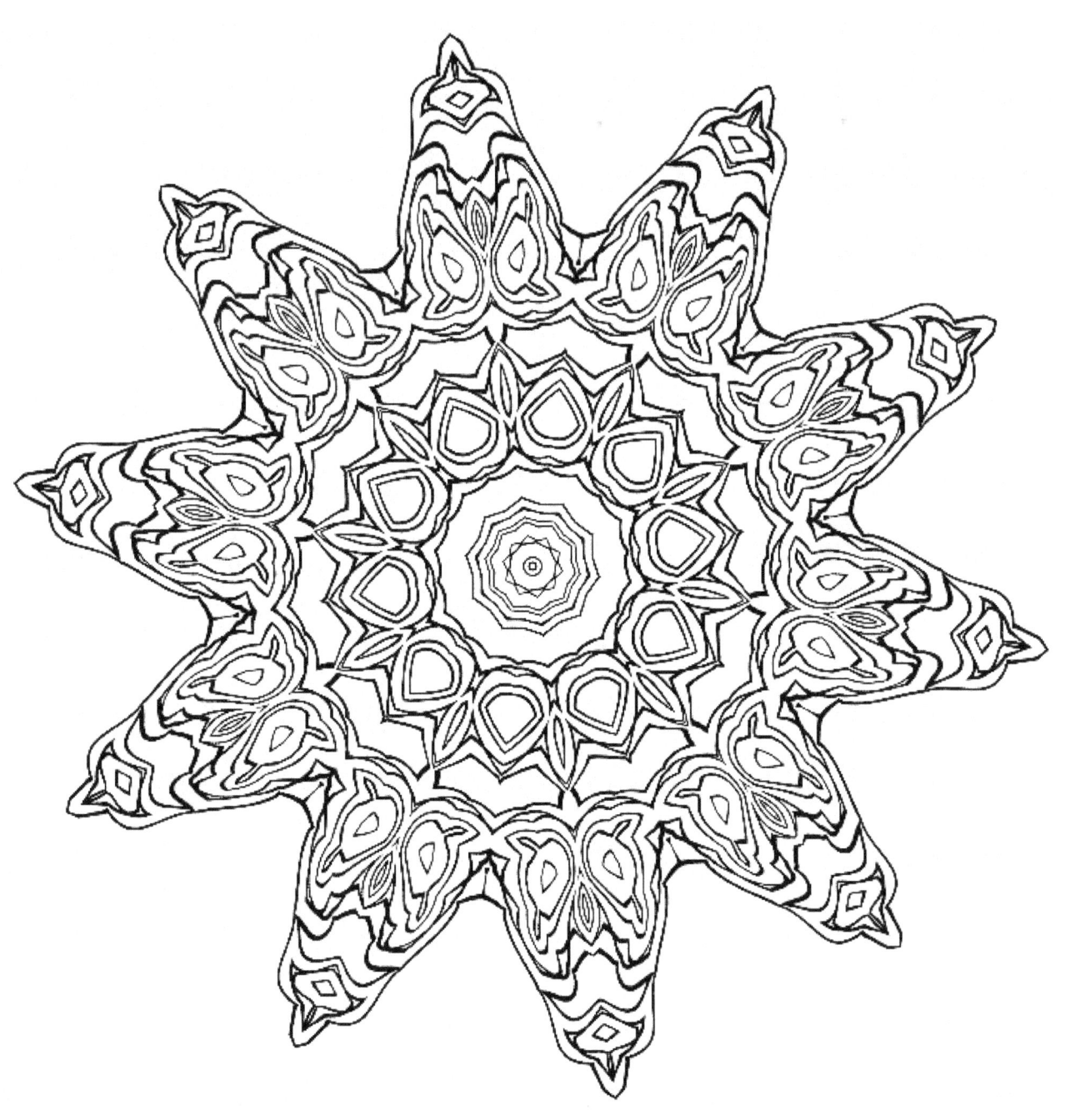

Totem Star

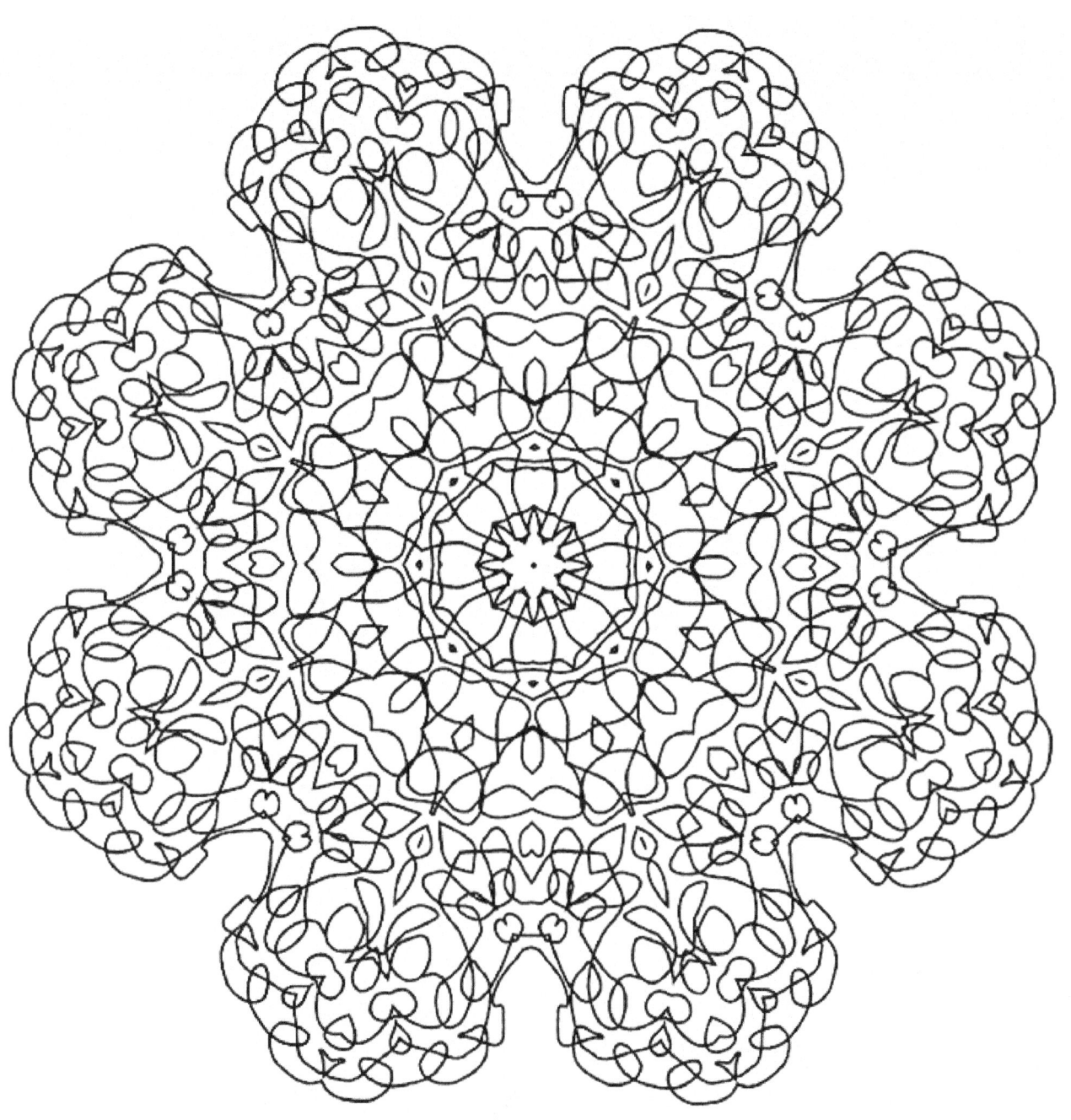

Vine Covered Ruins

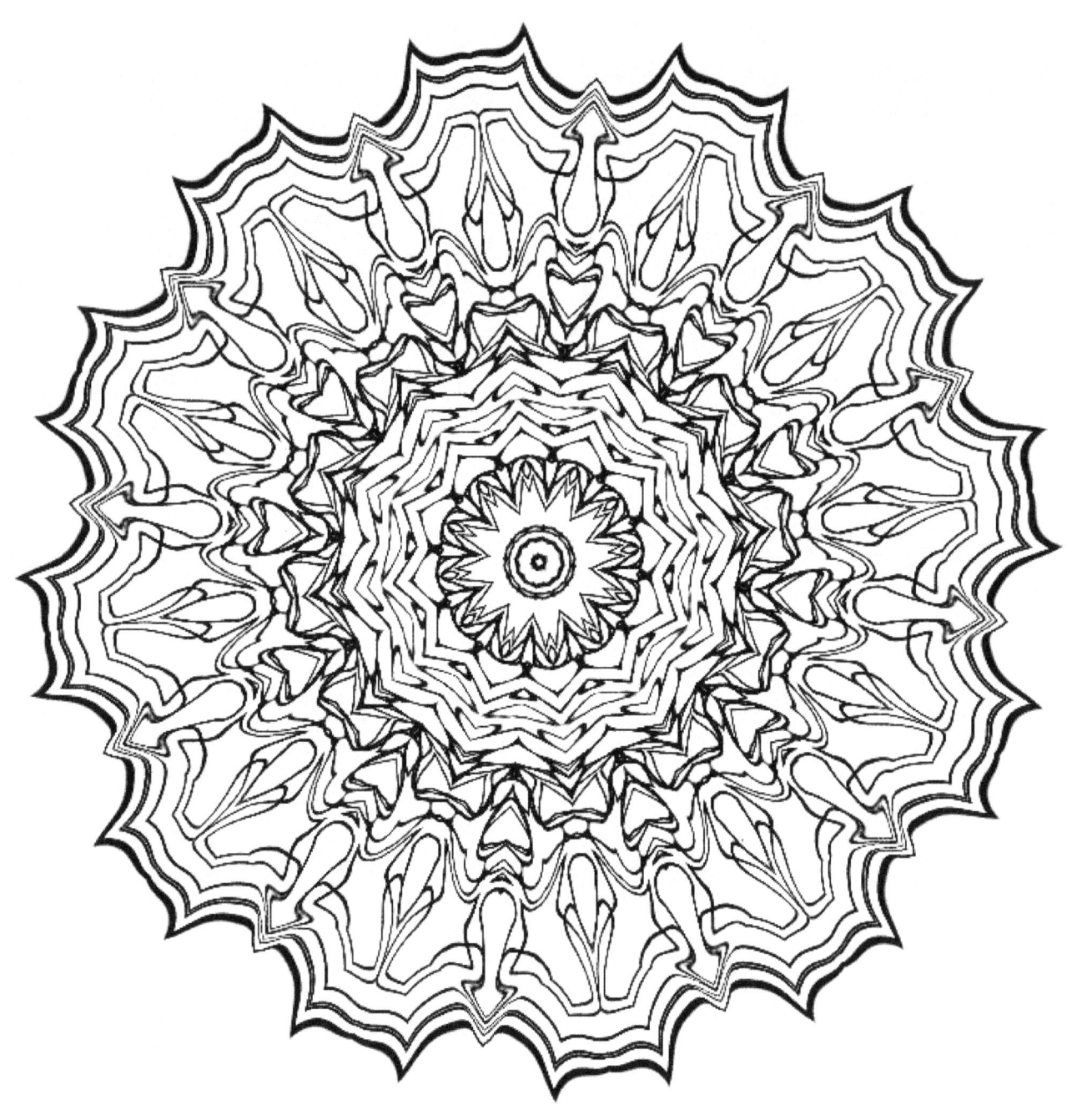

Woven

www.ingramcontent.com/pod-product-compliance
Lightning Source LLC
Chambersburg PA
CBHW080627190526
45169CB00009B/3310